NEW MEXICO BEER

A History of Brewing in
the Land of Enchantment

Jon C. Stott

AMERICAN PALATE

Published by American Palate
A Division of The History Press
Charleston, SC 29403
www.historypress.net

Copyright © 2014 by Jon C. Stott
All rights reserved

First published 2014

Manufactured in the United States

ISBN 978.1.60949.814.6

Library of Congress CIP data applied for.

For Clare and Alberto, with whom I most enjoy sharing New Mexico's great beers.

CONTENTS

PREFACE

First, I wish to thank Jerry Roberts, my commissioning editor at The History Press, who enthusiastically accepted my proposal for a book on New Mexico breweries, offered wise counsel and patiently guided me through the process of writing and preparing the manuscript through to its submission. To Ryan Finn, who edited the manuscript and made many suggestions for the improvement of what I had written, I also say thank you. These people have made *New Mexico Beer* a better book.

I wish to thank all the brewpub and brewery owners and brewers who graciously took time to answer my many questions, to show me their facilities and to offer me samples of their very good beers. Two people in particular have been exceptionally helpful: Christopher Goblet, executive director of the New Mexico Brewers Guild, and Bob Evaleth, the president of the Socorro Historical Society. As always, my daughter offered constant support and frequently offered to assist me in the liquid research that goes into writing a book about beer.

I read many newspaper and magazine articles and books about the beer and the craft beer movement. Three of the most valuable are Garrett Oliver, ed., *The Oxford Companion to Beer* (New York: Oxford University Press, 2011); Maureen Ogle, *Ambitious Brew: The Story of American Beer* (Orlando, FL: Harcourt, 2006); and Tom Acitelli, *The Audacity of Hops: The History of America's Craft Beer Revolution* (Chicago: Chicago Review Press, 2013). Donna Blake Birchell's *New Mexico Wine: An Enchanting History* (Charleston, SC: The

History Press, 2013) provided a very helpful introduction to New Mexico's other major beverage industry. The blog of the Dark Side Brew Crew (www. nmdarksidebrewcrew.com) provided regular updates on the beers offered by New Mexico breweries and brewpubs.

EXPLORING THE "FRONTIER OF BEER"

Y ou," said my friend who loves to use big words, "are a loca-cervezaphile." Not being familiar with the word, I didn't know whether to be insulted or flattered, so I asked for a definition. He explained that a locavore was a person who, as often as possible, ate food grown close to home. A cervezaphile was someone who loved good beer. "You not only like good beer, but you're always telling me that you like to buy beer as close to where it's brewed as possible. So I've decided to call you a loca-cervezaphile."

I was flattered, and I agreed. For well over a decade, I've made a point of buying beer brewed in the state or province in which I was living. And when I travel, I always stop at a liquor store, carefully read the labels of the beers and chose a six-pack of something that's local. I either take it to my destination or, as is most frequently the case, enjoy a couple of bottles at the night's motel.

In 2001, I began spending the winter months at my daughter's home in New Mexico and, of course, engaged in my "loca-cervezaphile" activities. What I noticed when I returned each winter was that the number of New Mexico beers available had increased considerably and that nearly all of them were very good.

Several years ago, I wrote *Beer Quest West*, a book about the craft breweries, brews and brewers of western Canada. When (after a very early and cold autumn in Edmonton, Alberta) I decided to move permanently to Albuquerque, I thought that I would expand my investigations into the beer culture of New Mexico, what the New Mexico Brewers Guild calls the "Frontier of Beer." In preparation for my explorations of this frontier, I searched the Internet for a guidebook about New Mexico breweries and beer. I'd seen others for the Pacific Northwest, Michigan and Connecticut, places I have visited frequently, but there wasn't a book for New Mexico. I did, however, discover that The History Press had published beer histories/guides for several cities and states in its "American Palate" series. It would, I thought, be fun to write one about New Mexico, becoming the Lewis and Clark of my explorations of the "Frontier of Beer"—not just learning during my travels but also sharing my discoveries with others.

The people at The History Press agreed, and in late 2012, I began my explorations. I visited breweries in big cities and small towns, as well as some that weren't even in small towns. I discovered breweries in a late nineteenth-century butcher shop, a 1920s J.C. Penney's department store, a 1940s blacksmith shop in a log cabin, an outbuilding in a Benedictine monastery and many converted warehouses. The brewers I met had come to the profession from formal training and home-brewing. One was a music teacher in his life before joining the brewing business, another was a real estate broker and a third was a stay-at-home mother. Several had been computer programmers and technicians. But all shared two common characteristics: they loved making beer and strove to make the best beer they could.

I sampled a variety of styles of beer. Every brewery had its version of India pale ale, and most of them had an amber ale or a stout. But I also tried a Dortmunder Export, a California common beer, some saisons, a kolsch and even a beer that included prickly pear cactus as one of its ingredients. I read many newspaper and magazine articles and several books about the brewing of beer, beer styles and beer history. And I made copious notes.

New Mexico Beer contains the results of my visits and research. After an introductory chapter presenting the two eras of New Mexico brewing history—from the 1850s to Prohibition and then the years since 1988, when Santa Fe Brewing Company opened—there are profiles on each of the thirty-three New Mexico breweries that were operational at the end of September 2013, my cut-off date. These essays are grouped in chapters for seven regional areas of the state—three for Albuquerque (west of Interstate 40, east of Interstate 40 and the surrounding areas). There are chapters for Santa Fe, Taos and for breweries scattered in the northern and in southern parts of the state. Each essay presents the background of the brewery, profiles of owners and brewers and descriptions of the main beers, along with some unusual ones. An appendix provides descriptions of the main beer styles, along with the names of some New Mexico examples of each style.

In these essays, two abbreviations are frequently used. "ABV" refers to the percentage of alcohol by volume. The pale American lagers of the megabrewers are around 5 percent ABV; beers categorized as "double" or "imperial" are above 7 percent ABV. "IBU" refers to International Bitterness Unit, which is used to measure the level of bitterness the hops contribute to a beer. India pale ales are frequently the strongest, often reaching the level of 100 IBUs. The beers of the megabrewers are extremely low in IBUs, sometimes as low as 15 percent. "Barrel" is another frequently used term. As the basic unit of measure in the beer industry, a barrel is thirty-one gallons—that's fifty-four six-packs, with three bottles left over.

In my travels throughout New Mexico's "Frontier of Beer," I learned that the brewing industry is figuratively, as well as literally, extremely fluid. I heard confirmations and rumors of new breweries opening and of others closing, of brewers moving from one place to another and of brewers experimenting and discovering ways of making new beers with old (and sometimes new) ingredients. The information in *New Mexico Beer* is current to the end of September 2013 and sometimes beyond. However, I continue to travel, explore and learn. My website (www.beerquestwest.com) will contain updates on the New Mexico beer scene, along with accounts of my beer travels in other areas, profiles of interesting beer people I have met and descriptions of new, imaginative beers I have encountered.

Cheers! May you enjoy exploring the "Frontier of Beer" as much as I did.

CHAPTER 1
BREWING IN NEW MEXICO

A BRIEF HISTORY

Although Native Americans may have brewed a beer-like corn beverage at least two centuries before the Spaniards began their occupation of what is now the American Southwest, New Mexico's first breweries did not begin operation until shortly after the middle of the nineteenth century. Since the early seventeenth century, when Spaniards planted the first vines, wine had been produced, and by the 1880s, New Mexico Territory was the fifth-largest wine producer in the United States.

The early and continued popularity of wine can be attributed to the importance of the beverage in Hispanic culture and to the facts that it had a relatively long life when bottled and could be fairly easily transported. Beer, by contrast, was a product of the British Isles and northern Europe, and until 1848, when New Mexico officially became a United States territory, there were few "Anglos," as British and northern Europeans were known, in the Southwest. Not only was there not much of a market for beer, but the area's climate also made brewing difficult; the considerable distances between population centers made transporting the easily spoiled beer nearly impossible as well.

An 1855 newspaper report of a Santa Fe brewery destroyed by a flood provides the earliest record of a brewery in the new territory. During the 1860s, three breweries operated in Santa Fe, as well as one in Las Cruces and one in Sapello (just north of Las Vegas). In the 1870s, three breweries opened in Lincoln, two in Santa Fe and one each in Fort Union, Golondrinas, Elizabethtown and Silver City. The next decade saw openings in Georgetown, Albuquerque, Deming, Fort Stanton and Kingston. Only two breweries began business in the 1890s, one in Mogollon and another in Las Vegas. In the first decade of the twentieth century, there were brewery openings in Bland, Albuquerque and Las Vegas. After A.H. Reingruber Brewing Company of Las Vegas began making beer in 1909, it would be another seventy-nine years before a new brewery opened in the Land of Enchantment.

A survey of a list of early New Mexico breweries reveals three interesting facts. First, although Albuquerque, Las Cruces, Santa Fe and Las Vegas, all towns along the Santa Fe Trail and later the railroads, had their share of breweries, many others operated in places that are now ghost towns or, at best, tiny villages. Mogollon, Bland, Elizabethtown, Georgetown, Kingston and Sapello were boomtowns, built during the silver and, to a lesser extent, gold rushes in the later part of the nineteenth century and disappearing or dwindling to a few dozen people when the boom ended. Forts Stanton and Union protected area settlers from hostile native peoples and acted as supply centers, as did Golondrinas and Lincoln.

Second, most of the nineteenth- and early twentieth-century breweries did not operate for extended periods. Thirteen of them lasted for three years or less and four for only one year each. When the mines closed and the workers departed, the breweries had no reason to exist. Moreover, during the 1880s—when refrigeration and pasteurization became important for the preservation of beer, major railroads reached the main centers and spur lines often connected these centers to the boomtowns—beer could more easily be transported and delivered unspoiled to the smaller places.

Third, a larger number of these New Mexico breweries were owned and/or operated by German immigrants or their first- and second-generation descendants. Beginning in the 1840s, German-born or German-trained brewers established the breweries in the Midwest that would dominate the American brewing industry and make lagers the major American style up to the present day. What became the Pabst Brewing Company was formed in Milwaukee in 1844, Schlitz in 1858 in the same city, Strohs in Detroit in 1850 and Anheuser-Busch in St. Louis in 1860. In New Mexico, Koening, Loeb, Kleiner, Ehrmann, Schwenk, Weber, Leininger, Reingruber, Kirschner, Probst, Fischer, Hauswald and Hammel are among the German names that appear in the lists of brewers and breweries. They undoubtedly created lagers, including the recently developed pilsner style. Brewing must have been a challenge, given the fact that lagers require much lower brewing temperatures and longer fermentation periods than ales. There must have been great numbers of suds consumed that were barely palatable to thirsty workers.

Between the years 1900 and 1918, when Prohibition began in New Mexico, only six breweries operated in the state and only two for the entire period: Illinois Brewery of Socorro and Southwestern Brewery and Ice Company in Albuquerque. By the early twentieth century, the major midwestern breweries had refrigerator cars, and rail transportation was so extensive that their beers were available in large parts of New Mexico. Significantly, both Illinois and Southwestern had their own refrigeration plants and were, to an extent, able to offer alternatives to beer imported from outside the area.

Southwestern Brewery and Ice Company was formed in 1888 by Don and Henry Rankin, formerly of Lawrence, Kansas. By the early part of the twentieth century, the brewery was one of Albuquerque's largest employers. More than thirty thousand barrels of beer were produced annually and shipped in the company's refrigerated rail cars throughout the Southwest. Its most famous beer, Glorietta Lager, achieved almost cult status, and in the early twenty-first century, Glorietta items command high prices among collectors of brewery memorabilia. Although no beer was produced at the Albuquerque plant after New Mexico established Prohibition in 1918, Glorietta was contract-brewed out of state in the late 1930s. The facility produced ice until the 1980s and currently stands unoccupied at the edge of downtown Albuquerque.

Illinois Brewery of Socorro was named after a brewery in Lebanon, Illinois, that had been founded in early 1850s by Jacob Hammel, who had emigrated from Germany with his friend Eberhard Anheuser, who later cofounded the famous brewery in St. Louis. In the 1880s, Hammel's son, William, who had moved to Socorro for health reasons, decided to found a brewery in the New Mexico town. Located close to the railroad and having ice-making facilities, the brewery prospered when others in nearby mining communities failed. However, like Southwest, it did not brew beer when Prohibition ended, although the plant continued to make soft drinks and ice for several more years.

Both Southwestern Brewery and Illinois Brewery, along with the many more breweries that did not make it out of the 1930s and early 1940s, were victims not only of the Depression and World War II but also of the incredible expansion in both production and distribution of such midwestern brewing giants as Schlitz, Millers, Anheuser-Busch and Pabst. The enormous breweries of these companies could produce beer far more cheaply than small regional ones. In addition, they had enormous advertising budgets and

Only the sign atop a vacant building at the edge of downtown Albuquerque indicates that before Prohibition it was the home of the largest brewery in the Southwest. *Courtesy the author.*

sophisticated transportation and distribution systems. In the 1950s and later, Anheuser-Busch, Hamm's, Schlitz, Falstaff and Pabst established plants in California, all of them relatively close to the New Mexico market. In addition, Coors, the large regional brewery located in Golden, Colorado, established a distribution network in New Mexico.

In the two decades preceding 1988, when Santa Fe Brewing Company became the first new brewery to open in New Mexico since 1909, there had been a small but significant change in the brewing industry and in consumers' tastes. Beginning in California and then spreading northward into Oregon and Washington and eastward into Colorado, small breweries began to introduce older, almost forgotten styles of ales. The movement began in 1965 when Fritz Maytag, a member of the family noted for the production of appliances, purchased the failing Anchor Brewing Company. He reintroduced "steam beer," a style dating back to gold rush days, then a porter and an India pale ale. All of these styles had a robustness of flavor lacking in the virtually indistinguishable lagers created by the megabrewers. Within a decade, India pale ale, noted for its abundant use of bittering and aroma/flavoring hops, was demanding attention from drinkers whose only alternative to pale American lagers had been ales imported from the British Isles and lagers from Europe.

New Mexican beer drinkers traveling to Europe, the West Coast and to Colorado (after 1980, when Boulder Brewing opened) began to discover and appreciate the new flavors of the beers created in what were variously known as cottage, boutique, micro and craft breweries. As the 1980s wore on, an increasing number of craft brews became available in stores, bars and restaurants in New Mexico. Soon many people began to ask, "Why aren't there beers like this being brewed in New Mexico?" One of the people asking was Mike Levis, a horse rancher who lived just outside Santa Fe and who owned a business that supplied bottles to the growing number of New Mexico wineries.

Levis took action to end the situation. He purchased a used seven-barrel brewing system from Boulder Brewing and in 1988 opened Santa Fe Brewing Company. During the first year of operation, it produced five hundred barrels of beer, which he sold in bottles and draft to accounts in the Santa Fe and Albuquerque regions. The styles—an American wheat ale, a pale ale and a nut brown ale—were what might now be called "crossover" or "entry-level" beers, but they were different from anything that had ever been brewed in New Mexico. Santa Fe Brewing grew slowly but gradually acquired a loyal customer base. Twenty-five years later, the company was producing more than twenty thousand barrels annually and had accounts throughout the Southwest.

In 2013, the brewery celebrated its twenty-fifth anniversary in a way that would not have been possible in 1988. Saison 88 was a commemorative ale packaged in cans. A quarter of a century earlier, few beer drinkers would have heard of this Belgian style, and had they been offered a taste of it, they might have criticized it as being too unusual—nothing like the pale American lagers with which they were comfortable. It certainly wouldn't have been offered in cans. Because of their limited production, most early craft brewers could not have afforded the expense of installing a canning line and purchasing large quantities of cans. Moreover, many craft brewers and craft beer drinkers associated cans with products of the megabrewers and felt that craft beers should only be served on draft or in bottles.

During the more than twenty-five years that Santa Fe Brewing Company has operated and grown, fifty-seven more microbreweries and brewpubs have opened in New Mexico. Of these, only thirty-three were still brewing in the autumn of 2013. In 1989, Embudo Station, a restaurant south of

The state-of-the-art brewery adjacent to Interstate 25 is the third home of New Mexico's longest-running and largest craft brewery. The brewery began operations in 1988 in a converted horse barn near Galisteo. *Courtesy the author.*

Taos, next to the Rio Grande, began serving beer that had been brewed just a few hundred yards away by the Sangre de Cristo Brewery, operated by Steve Eskeback. Although the restaurant continued to brew its own beer for close to a decade and a half, Eskeback departed in 1992 to start his own establishment in Taos: Eske's Brew Pub & Eatery. Still open, it is the longest-operating brewpub in New Mexico. During this period, nine other breweries opened, four in Albuquerque and one each in Santa Fe, Tijeras, Mesilla, Las Cruces and Elephant Butte. Of these, Il Vicino Brewing, which began making its own beer in 1994, is the lone survivor.

During the last few years of the twentieth century, the country saw both a rapid expansion in the number of breweries opening and in the number going out of business. In New Mexico, between 1996 and 1999, nineteen breweries began business, while eight closed their doors. Not surprisingly, Albuquerque, the state's biggest city, and its neighboring communities led in the number of openings with nine, five of which had gone out of business by the turn of the century. However, the four-year period also saw the establishment of six brewpubs that still remain favorite dining and drinking spots for New Mexicans. Blue Corn Brewery began business in Santa Fe in 1996 and in Albuquerque in 1999. In 1996, Kellys opened in Albuquerque, High Desert Brewing in Las Cruces and Second Street in Santa Fe. Turtle Mountain opened in Rio Rancho in 1999. In addition, the state's second and third production breweries began business—Sierra Blanca in Carrizozo (1996) and Tractor in Los Lunas (1999).

Between 2000 and 2007, seven new breweries opened, only two of which still operate. During the same period, ten closed. One of the survivors was The Wellhead, a brewpub in Artesia, in the oil country of southeastern New Mexico, a part of the state where pale American lagers, particularly the so-called "King of Beers," had ruled supreme. The other was Abbey Brewing, which had small test breweries at Benedictine monasteries first in Pecos and later outside Abiquiu and had the bulk of its brewing done at the Sierra Blanca Brewery in Moriarty. It was the first monastery brewery to operate in the United States since Prohibition.

New Mexico's brewers have been consistently recognized and honored on a national level, most notably at the annual Great American Beer Festival (GABF). Since 1991, when Santa Fe Nut Brown Ale was awarded a bronze medal, New Mexico beers have won forty-three Great American Beer Festival medals, twelve of them gold. The styles range from chile beer to kolsch, Dortmunder, IPA and more. Nine of the medals have been earned for brown ales. In 2013, New Mexico was one of the top award winners, earning eight medals—two golds, four silvers and two bronzes.

CHAPTER 2
ALBUQUERQUE, WEST OF INTERSTATE 25

BACK ALLEY DRAFT HOUSE

215 Central Avenue NW, Albuquerque, 87102
505-766-8590
Taproom: At the brewery.

In 2012, Joaquin Garofalo and Nilo Gonzales, the owners of New York Pizza Department, were considering what to do with a large room behind the kitchen of their downtown Albuquerque restaurant. "We used to book private parties into the space, but we needed to do something that would increase our business." That's when they realized that there wasn't a really good place to drink craft beer in the busy center of the city. And so the idea for Back Alley Draft House was born. The backroom was outfitted with a handsome bar, a foosball table, a dartboard, a jukebox decorated in 1950s style, television sets, a small outdoor patio and more than twenty taps for dispensing beer.

There was also a one-barrel nano-brewing system—the various vessels of which were placed in vacant spaces of the pizza restaurant's kitchen. "It was important for people to know that we were a brewery," Nilo Gonzalez explained. Being able to offer its own, brewed-on-premises ales gave Back

Alley an advantage over other restaurants in the vicinity. With only a small brewing system and limited space to age beer, the owners could only have a small number of styles on tap at once time. However, by installing guest taps, they could expand their range of offerings to include beers from New Mexico and out-of-state breweries.

When Back Alley opened in the late spring of 2012, two men handled the brewing duties. John Soens, a partner of Garofalo and Gonzales, was a lover of Belgian-style beers and had made trips to Europe just to drink Belgian brews. The first beer he offered to Back Alley customers was Cali Girl Cherry Wheat, designed to be something that was different yet easy on the palate. Soens's offerings were complemented by the creations of Majin Garcia, an award-winning home-brewer. His most popular beer was the Maple's Shade, an imperial stout using Belgian Candi syrup as well as maple flavoring.

Late in 2012, Addison Poth became the managing director of the draft house and soon after took over all the brewing. A graduate in business from Texas A&M University, he discovered that there was more out there than pale American lagers when, at age sixteen, he tried Blue Moon, a Belgian-style wheat beer manufactured by a Coors subsidiary. He learned the art of home-brewing from his father, won a gold medal at the New Mexico State Fair for his summer ale—which featured lemon zest and ginger root—and then assumed home-brewing duties in his college residence.

During his first year at Back Alley, Poth brewed many styles, developing more than thirty recipes, including an IPA, a pale ale, a java stout, a raspberry blond, a barley wine, an imperial red, an imperial porter and an imperial pumpkin ale. He called one of his most interesting creations White Ryno, a Belgian white-rye hybrid. "We've spent our first year tweaking recipes, working to get just the taste we wanted and making sure there was a consistency from batch to batch," he explained. "And we're listening very carefully to the feedback we're getting from our customers." With that information, he will establish a core list of beers that will always be on tap, along with seasonal offerings and brews from such other craft breweries as Marble, Chama River and Il Vicino.

In January 2014, Poth traveled to Berlin, Germany, to begin formal training in brewing. Upon his return, he will be establishing his core list and developing plans for the construction of a fifteen-barrel, off-site brewing system.

BOSQUE BREWING COMPANY

8900 San Mateo Boulevard NE, Suite 1, Albuquerque, 87113
505-433-3889, www.bosquebrewing.com
Taprooms: At the brewery and at 106 Gerrard Boulevard SE, Albuquerque (opening in the summer of 2014).

When Gabe Jensen, Kevin Jameson and Jotham Michnovicz decided that they wanted to form their own business, they discussed and rejected several ideas before Jensen suggested that they start a microbrewery. "The craft beer business was booming in New Mexico. And when I heard that Ted Rice of Marble Brewery had said that he could sell a lot more beer if only he had the equipment to brew more, I realized there was room for another brewery."

The trio decided that the industrial area in northwest Albuquerque would be a good location for their proposed brewery. The area had no breweries or taprooms, it was close to the Balloon Fiesta Park and it had more than enough potential customers who worked at nearby businesses. But there were two big obstacles the trio had to overcome before their dream could become a reality. They had to come up with the financing to build a brewery, and they had to learn how to brew beer.

Their application for a small business loan was turned down, so they applied to Accion New Mexico, Arizona and Colorado—a nonprofit organization that provides loans to small startup businesses—and were accepted. "They liked our business plan and provided us with $100,000, which was just what we needed."

Overcoming the second hurdle involved a long process of learning—discovering how to brew by trial and error. "We knew what we liked, and we knew what our friends liked," Gabe remembered, "but we didn't know how to make it. So we bought a pilot system and began. I was 'appointed' head brewer by my partners. My first batch, an ESB, was a disaster. But we kept at it, finding what worked and then learning how to achieve successful results consistently."

They scheduled the opening of the new brewery, named Bosque Brewing (a reference to the wooded area bordering the nearby Rio Grande), for late October 2012. A friend devised an unusual way of publicizing the brewery's impending arrival. He created three short "commercials" that he posted on YouTube. Entitled "Down with the King," the series of commercials traced the overthrow of a self-styled superhero called Beer King, who strides arrogantly into the new brewery, crowded with people who have come to the grand opening. His boorish behavior, topped by his placing a crown on his head, is denounced. "America is a democracy. There are no kings here," Jensen explained. "Flavor is boss."

At first, Bosque Brewing offered four different beers on a regular basis. Kindling, a 4.4 percent ABV golden ale that uses wheat, is designed as an entry-level, crossover beer. Cumulus is a whopping 7.0 percent ABV ale that offers a new take on New Mexico's most popular microbrewed style, IPA. It also uses wheat, which gives the brew the haze that led to its name. True to the IPA style, it is hoppy, registering 70 International Bitterness Units (IBU). The other two—Mellow Brit, an English-style brown ale, and Olde Bosky Porter—have since been discontinued.

Four new regulars have been added. Driftwood Oatmeal Stout replaced Olde Bosky. Brewer's Boot Amber Ale (5.8 percent ABV) is described as having biscuit, roasted caramel and earthy notes. Ember IPA (90 IBUs and 6.1 percent ABV) is a dry-hopped beer that Jensen described as being a hybrid of English and American styles. "We use English malts and American hops." Scotia Scotch is a "wee heavy," a style noted for its malty sweetness. At 8.4 percent ABV, it is Bosque's strongest year-round offering.

BROKEN BOTTLE BREWERY

9421 Coors Boulevard NW, Suite K, Albuquerque, 87114
505-890-8777, www.brokenbottlebrewery.com
Taproom: At the brewery.

The story of the founding of Broken Bottle, Albuquerque's first West Side brewery, is a familiar one. Chris Chavez and Donavan Lane were high school home-brewing buddies who decided to turn their hobby into a small business. "At first, we thought we'd open a home-brew supply store," Donavan Lane remembered. "But there were already two in Albuquerque, so we decided to open a microbrewery."

For startup funds, they pooled their own savings, along with loans and donations from friends and family, and also opened an account on Kickstarter, an Internet site that helps small businesses and organizations raise money. Their plan was simple: offer donors various premiums for their contributions. The premiums ranged from logo stickers of the brewery to merchandise such as T-shirts and mugs, as well as name plaques on taproom bar stools and chairs. The campaign raised a total of $8,691.

For their location, Lane and Chavez chose a strip mall on Coors Boulevard, a very busy north–south road on Albuquerque's rapidly expanding West Side, and started to build their brewery in a space that had formerly been an auto machine shop. They constructed a small (two-barrel) brewing system with inexpensive plastic fermenting vessels and built the chairs and tables for the taproom. Having a pizza shop and a takeout sushi restaurant in the same complex was an added bonus. Allowing patrons to bring in food from these establishments would spare the owners of the new brewery the expense of providing restaurant services. (Later, they contracted with Poco's, a well-known Albuquerque maker of smoked meats, to cater a limited menu that includes snacks and sandwiches.)

The two partners had tossed around many names before settling on the unusual one of Broken Bottle. "It represents our background. We're not formally trained. When we home-brewed, we made a lot of mistakes, and a lot of bottles broke after we put the beer in them."

Lane and Chavez wanted to give Broken Bottle the feeling of a neighborhood pub, "a place where people could drop by for a pint after work or in the evening and on weekends, or bring in a growler to be filled and taken home." There is only one television, but there is a small stage for musicians. There are stand-up comedy evenings, along with Trivial Pursuit tournaments. "We want people to have something more to do than just show up and drink beer."

Since opening in April 2012, Lane and Chavez have offered more than thirty different beers. Usually there are ten styles on tap—six regulars and four seasonals. "You could say our motto is 'Try new things,'" Lane explained. "We aren't afraid to push the envelope. We're becoming noted for our unusual seasonals; they sell out very quickly."

The year-round beers include two under 5 percent ABV: Steamy Lawyer, a California common or steam beer, an introductory beer "with much more body than Bud Light"; and June Bug, a summer ale that is like a blond ale but with lemon zest and paradise seed (a peppery Mediterranean spice) as additives. "It started as a seasonal but was so popular that we made it a regular." AFD (as in Albuquerque Fire Department) Red is a 5.4 percent ABV ale in the American style. The brewery's top seller, Mulligan Stout, is an Irish stout. "People expect something like Guinness, but ours is much more robust at 5.7 percent ABV." Year 2 IPA is Broken Bottle's version of

New Mexico's most popular craft beer style. "Many breweries try to make their IPAs as hoppy as possible. We want ours to be mellower, with a hop-malt balance." The 6.6 percent ABV ale is the brewery's number-two seller. The Incident Black IPA is the strongest regular offering, at 7.2 percent ABV.

Broken Bottle's imaginative flair is seen in the unusual list of additives it has included during the first two years of brewing: fennel and caraway seeds (Xico Sauve), New Mexico red chile (Anomole Stout), watermelon (Wise Ass Watermelon Wheat), sunflower seeds (Sol Rosenberg Ale), rosemary (Rosemary's Baby) and cranberry (Tom Selleck Ale).

CHAMA RIVER BREWING COMPANY

4939 Pan American Freeway, Albuquerque, 87109
505-342-1800, www.chamariverbrewery.com
Taprooms: *At the brewery and at Chama River Microbar, 106 Second Street SW, Albuquerque.*

Albuquerque's Chama River Brewing Company opened in 1999 as Blue Corn Brewery, a sister brewpub to the Santa Fe Blue Corn Brewery established in 1997 by the Santa Fe Dining group. Located just off Interstate 25 in northern Albuquerque, it was an adobe-style restaurant specializing in New Mexico–style food and brewing its own beer. The beer styles were what are now called "main stream craft," ranging from light to dark and neither too high in alcohol nor too hoppy. Two of initial brewer Ted Rice's beers won medals at the Great American Beer Festival. In 2002, Get Off My Bock was awarded a silver medal in the bock category; one year later, Atomic Blonde took gold in the German-style kolsch category.

However, while the beers garnered awards, Blue Corn Albuquerque's food menu, while very good, wasn't that well received. There were just too many Southwest, Mexican and New Mexican restaurants in Albuquerque. It became evident that Blue Corn needed to reinvent itself to stand out. In May 2004, Santa Fe Dining's corporate office announced that it was developing a new concept and that the restaurant would be completely renovated. A different menu would be created and several new beer styles added. A few months later, it was reopened as Chama River Brewing Company, an upscale gastropub.

Chama River Brewing, which opened as Blue Corn Brewery in 1999, is Albuquerque's first gastro-brewpub. *Courtesy the author.*

A very important part of the renovations was the enlargement of the brew house so that a larger number of styles could be created. "It gave us opportunities to experiment, to offer a number of one-offs. But most of all, I had an opportunity to focus on IPAs, and I haven't looked back," Ted Rice remembered. In 2004, his Rye-On won a gold medal at the Great American Beer Festival. During the brewery's first year as Chama River, Rice and his assistants created more than thirty different styles or versions of styles. Seven of these were pale ales or IPAs, three were Belgian styles and eight were imperial beers with alcoholic content of more than 7 percent. In its reinvention, Chama River was at the forefront of the movement that saw unfamiliar and often strong beer styles become an important aspect of the craft brewing industry in New Mexico.

In 2008, Rice left Chama River to create Marble Brewery. Jeff Erway, his replacement, had worked as his assistant and continued the medal-winning tradition. Erway's kellerbier and stout won GABF bronze medals in 2008 and 2009, respectively, while his Three Dog Night Baltic Porter won a gold in 2010. In 2011, he, too, left Chama River to start his own production brewery and taproom, La Cumbre.

Located among a cluster of other restaurants and near a multiplex cinema, Chama River is identified by the large grain silo standing just south of the building. Patrons coming into the restaurant pass by an outdoor patio with a wood-burning fireplace The medals won by the brewers in regional, national and international contests are displayed along one of the lobby walls. The five-barrel brew house is visible through floor-to-ceiling windows behind the bar. Although it is relatively small for a commercial system, "We are able to keep up with demand," current brewer Justin Hamilton explained, "because we have eighteen bright [conditioning] tanks in our cold room."

While the menu includes such New Mexico staples as chile nachos and a green chile burger, there are interesting twists such as red chile–glazed duck legs and green chile and ale fondue. But there are also baby back ribs, Mediterranean chicken, lobster-basil mashed potatoes, truffled blue cheese fries and crème brûlée. The full-service bar offers specialty wines from around the world and more than a dozen types of martinis.

Justin Hamilton began visiting Chama River when it was Blue Corn, discovering that its amber and stout beers had so much more flavor than the bland American lagers he had been drinking. "I worked with Chama River as a waiter for a year and realized that I wanted to be on the brewery side of the operations," he remembered. When a delivery job at Santa Fe's Blue Corn became available, he took it as a means of getting his foot in the door. "Daniel Jaramillo was the brewer there, and he gave me the opportunity to work in the brewery. I said I'd do it on my off hours and for free. But he paid me." Jaramillo taught Hamilton, who had never home-brewed, the basics of brewing.

In addition to Jaramillo, Hamilton counts Ted Rice and Jeff Erway, for whom he worked at Marble and Chama River, as his mentors. "Ted taught me many of the techniques of brewing and introduced me to the tricks of brewing barley wines and Belgian-style beers. He emphasized how important a good palate was for a brewer." From Erway, he learned how to use hops in making IPAs. "He also taught me the importance of a healthy competitiveness among brewers. We all help each other, but when somebody does something really good, it encourages the rest of us to become better than we now are." Like his mentors Rice and Erway, Hamilton wants to establish his own brewery, something he hopes to do in late 2014.

Although Hamilton inherited the six core beers developed by Rice and Erway, he has tweaked each of them. Three—Class VI Lager, Broken Spoke Wheat Ale and Chama River Amber—are designed as crossover beers. The lager (5.0 percent alcohol by volume and 27 IBUs) started out as a German helles but has moved toward the German pilsner style. Light and dry, it uses German Tettnanger, Magnum and Czech Saaz hops to give it a crisp bitterness and clean finish. Broken Spoke (5.5 percent ABV and 20 IBUs) is an American wheat ale with honey. Hamilton has made it less cloying and drier than most examples of the style. "It's a beer-drinker's beer," he said. "And it's also a good drink for people who aren't used to bitterness in their beer." Rio Chama Amber Ale (5.6 percent ABV and 20 IBUs) has been made to resemble a German alt, a traditional style noted for its balance between malts and hops. Although caramel malts are most noticeable, there are just enough Noble hops to provide a clean finish.

Rio Lodo Brown, a 5.5 percent ABV, is hoppier than its English counterparts, as its 30 IBU rating suggests. Chocolate and caramel malts give it a rich and roasted flavor, while the hops provide a clean finish. "Our brown can stand up with Moose Drool," Hamilton noted proudly, referring to a Montana brown that became very popular when it was first introduced into New Mexico. Sleeping Dog Stout (6.0 percent ABV and 25 IBUs), an oatmeal stout, is, in Hamilton's words, "chewy and roasty, with rich coffee and espresso flavors. It's a great dessert beer and cold weather warmer." A blend of oats provides a creamy smoothness.

Jackalope IPA, named after a mythical half-rabbit/half-antelope creature, is Chama River's most popular beer, outselling all others combined by a margin of two to one. At 110 IBUs, it is a real hop bomb and one "our knowledgeable drinkers love." Columbus, Crystal and Centennial hops provide citrusy and piney notes. "It's a beer that's constantly evolving," Hamilton remarked. "In Albuquerque, you've got to have a strong IPA, and the public expects you to keep up with what the others are doing."

Like his mentors and friendly competitors Rice and Erway, Hamilton enjoys crafting relatively unfamiliar and often very different styles that, to use Rice's words, "entertain both the brewer and the beer drinker." Some of his creations include Eternal Night, a foreign stout; Captain's Chair IPA; Cold Crush Kolsch; Shadow Boxer Black IPA; and the Beast of Bourbon, a barrel-aged imperial brown ale. Asked to name what he thought were some the most interesting and unusual beers he has made, he mentioned two. His bourbon cask cream ale was, as he termed it, "dosed" with vanilla and aged for fourteen months. "It had a complex mix of flavors, including vanilla, oak and caramel." His gingerbread wheat beer was spiked with sugar and ginger.

Speaking about his role as a brewer, Hamilton noted that he wanted his menu beers to be consistent, balanced and true to style and his different beers to be both well made and interesting. "Most important," he continued,

"I want to give the customer the experience of enjoying really good beer and a great place in which to enjoy it."

MARBLE BREWERY

111 Marble Avenue NW, Albuquerque, 87102
505-243-2739, www.marblebrewery.com
Taprooms: At the brewery and at 5740 Night Whisper Road NW, Albuquerque, and 505
Cerrillos Road, Santa Fe

In what used to be part of the parking lot north of Albuquerque's Marble Brewery stand three 120-barrel fermenters and a 120-barrel bright tank, all surrounded by a high chain link fence. They were installed between the late 2012 and late 2013 and are an indication of the success that Marble has enjoyed since opening in April 2008. In nearly all breweries, these pieces of equipment are found inside the brew house. But at Marble, demand for the beers has grown so much that earlier expansion had taken all the room inside, and further expansion had to be carried on outside the building. In its first six years of operation, Marble's production rose from 1,950 barrels per year to 10,750 barrels.

In 2007, three employees of the Santa Fe Dining group—Jeff Jinnett, the company's president; John Gozigian, the vice-president of operations; and Ted Rice, the award-winning brewer of the company's Chama River Brewing—decided to establish a production brewery. "We felt that the time was right for a combined production brewery and taproom in downtown Albuquerque," Jinnett said. "We'd seen how successful the downtown Chama River Tap Room was, even though it seated only twenty people. We didn't want a restaurant where people came to order a meal, along with a beer or two, eat and then leave. It would be more like a coffee shop in which they could relax and linger, reading, working on their laptops, playing board games or just visiting."

The old Starco Industrial Supply Warehouse and Showroom just north of downtown Albuquerque suited their needs almost perfectly. The warehouse could be transformed into a brew house, and the showroom could become the taproom. It was close enough to downtown that people could drop by for an after-work drink, and because the group had purchased two adjacent

Since it first opened in 2008, Marble Brewery has grown so much that, in a recent expansion, several brewing tanks had to be installed outside the building. *Courtesy the author.*

residential lots, there would be plenty of free parking. However, there was a problem: the building was more than fifty years old, and nothing was up to code. "We paid $400,000 for the building and $170,000 for the adjacent property," Jinnett reported, "but by the time we had brought everything up to code, bought and installed a brew house and renovated the spaces that would become the taproom and the offices, our startup costs were $1.7 million."

The initial plan was to shut down the Blue Corn brew house in Santa Fe, move the equipment to larger quarters in Albuquerque and, from there, brew for both Blue Corn and new Marble accounts. The plan changed: a new fifteen-barrel brew house was installed at the Albuquerque location and a taproom added. This proved to be a fortunate decision. Within three months, demand for Marble's product, in bottles and on draft, was so great that the brewery couldn't make enough to supply its own as well as Blue Corn's needs. The Santa Fe facility was quickly reactivated.

"We were a little anxious before we opened," Director of Operations John Gozigian remembers. "We felt confident that we'd succeed but thought that things might be quite slow at first." He needn't have worried; Marble's taproom was packed on opening day, April 23, 2008. On warm spring afternoons, people cycling to Marble found that space to attach bicycles to the chain link fence surrounding the patio area was at a premium. Gozigian estimated that the taproom was so successful that, at first, close to 90 percent of all sales were made there. "Even now," he said in late 2013, "sales at our taprooms account for nearly 20 percent of our business."

The popularity of the taproom did not abate, and new accounts continued to be created across the state. In 2009, Marble's first full year of operation, production rose to five thousand barrels and the next to eight thousand. A Santa Fe taproom opened in 2009, along with a third, on Albuquerque's West Side, in 2012. In 2011, a thirty-barrel system and more fermenters were installed, making elbowroom in the brew house scarce. In 2012, Marble began to can its IPA, becoming the second brewery in the state to use this form of packaging. In 2013, it added its Pilsner to the canned lineup. By the end of 2013, Marble products had become available throughout New Mexico and in Arizona and Colorado.

Asked what it meant to be operating a production brewery rather than a brewpub, Rice remarked, "We don't have to rely on the restaurant side of the operation. The focus is all about the beer." He did stress, however, that food is available at the taprooms. Snacks and sandwiches are catered by nearby restaurants, and patrons can phone out to have food delivered or can bring their own. At the downtown location, food trucks, vetted by Marble's management, park on the street beside the brewery, offering their wares.

Rice had gone to Roanoke College in Virginia to study sociology; however, one of his most valuable experiences was tasting his roommate's home-brew. When he returned home to Long Island after graduating, he took up the hobby himself. Soon he was working at a local brewpub. Then he studied at the American Brewers Guild in California and, after that, ran a brewpub in Florida. When he and his wife, Amberly, moved to Albuquerque, he joined the Blue Corn (later Chama River) brewing team, working in both Santa Fe and Albuquerque. By the time he left Chama River in late 2007 to participate in the founding of Marble, his beers at Blue Corn and Chama River had won two gold medals and a silver at the Great American Beer Festival.

Marble Brewery produces four beers on a year-round basis. (The number used to be larger, but demand for the "core four" has been so great that the brewery now focuses on these.) The simply named IPA, which has been the bestseller since the brewery's April 2008 opening, reflects Ted Rice's fascination with the many potentialities of hops—six varieties of which are used in the brew. "We strive for a rich, deep, citrusy, resinous hop flavor. It's hoppy and dry but not rough." At 6.8 percent ABV, it is a fairly strong beer. Marble Red is also both hoppy and relatively strong (6.5 percent ABV). "Our IPA was really good, but we wanted something else, something that was hoppy but different. It uses caramel malts, which give a chewy, toffee, nutty characteristic, but the Cascade hops offset the potential sweetness."

The two other regulars, lighter in both flavor and alcohol content, appeal to those craft beer drinkers who are not yet ready for the hoppier and more robust flavors of the IPA and the Red. Marble Pilsner (4.7 percent ABV), which has received a silver and a bronze medal at the Great American Beer Festival, is light in color, clean and refreshing. The other lighter regular, Wild Flower Wheat, uses local honey to create a subtle, slightly sweet difference from other versions of the popular American-style wheat beer.

Frequently available, but not in the regular core lineup, are an amber ale, an oatmeal stout, an imperial red ale (winner of a GABF silver medal), a double IPA and an imperial stout. "And," Rice noted, "we like to do different things, brews that will entertain us and our customers." The list of beers created by Marble during its first five years has reached more than eighty in number and includes several Belgian styles, sour and barrel-aged beers, along with a pumpkin porter and Thunder from Dortmunder (winner of a GABF bronze medal).

Perhaps the most interesting of the "entertaining" beers was a pair of brews released late in the summer of 2013. Heisenberg's Dark, a 6.5 percent ABV India Black Ale, and Walt's White Lie, a 7.5 percent India White Ale, were named after the central character in *Breaking Bad*, the extremely popular television series that was shot in and around Albuquerque. "The show had placed our beer in several episodes, and we wanted to say thank you," Rice explained. "The show gave international attention to Albuquerque, and when these beers were released, they gained a great deal of national attention."

Asked which of his beers he likes best, Rice gives a reply similar to that of a father of many children asked to name his favorite. "I love all my beers," he replied. "I nurture them all. My favorite one at a specific time depends on the weather, my mood, the food I'm eating, a lot of things. But at the end of the day, I'm always drawn to hops."

TRACTOR BREWING COMPANY

1800 Fourth Street NW, Albuquerque, 87102
505-243-6752; www.getplowed.com
Taprooms: At the brewery and at 118 Tulane Drive SE, Albuquerque.

In 1999, Herb Pluemer, who grew up on a Wisconsin dairy farm, opened a beer farm in the agricultural community of Los Lunas, New Mexico. The beer farm—most of us would call it a brewery or brew house—was set up in the same building that housed RIBS Hickory Pit Barbeque, a country-style restaurant he co-owned.

"Tractor," the name he gave his new business, reflected not only his agricultural background but also his childhood love of these farm machines and his later hobby of collecting and then restoring old tractors. A trained mechanic who owned Accurate Machine, Tool and related businesses in New Mexico, Pluemer placed many of his revitalized tractors around the restaurant/brewery, a move that not only caught the eye of passing motorists but also enticed many of them to stop, look at the equipment and then stay to enjoy the food and beer.

Mike Campbell, a onetime home-brewer who had previously worked for Wolf Canyon Brewing Company, a now-defunct Santa Fe brewery, acquired the title of "Beer Farmer." Newly filled kegs and bottles were called "the harvest." And the four initial beers bore agricultural names: Farmer's Tan Red Ale, Haymaker Honey Wheat, Double Plow Oatmeal Stout and Sod Buster Pale Ale. Advertising taglines for the beers included such admonitions as "Make hay while the sun shines, drink this anytime."

At first, Tractor flourished. Sales were brisk at the restaurant/taproom, and there were taps in other area restaurants; six-packs sold briskly in New Mexico and could even be found in such distant places as Oklahoma, New York and New Jersey.

But then, like other small farms, the beer farm threatened to become an endangered species. In 2008, Herb Pluemer considered closing down the business. That's when Sky Devore and David Hargis entered the picture. "I didn't know a great deal about beer. I had always been a Miller Lite person," she confessed. But she had a Master of Business Administration degree with a specialization in marketing and production management. "We needed a new business plan," she remembered. "We had the product, but we needed people to know about us."

Reinvigorating the beer farm, creating good harvests and increasing sales proved challenging. James Walton, who had replaced Campbell, moved on; the beer system became infected and resistant to attempts to sanitize it. One of the old tanks exploded, spilling gallons of "harvest" on the brewery floor. In the summer of 2010, Devore found a new brewer, David Hargis. He had home-brewed for ten years and worked in a home-brew supply shop, but this was his first professional brewing job.

Hargis installed a new brewing system and tweaked recipes. He added an IPA (Farmer's Almanac) to the list of year-round beers. "By this time, the

Although Tractor Brewing's Albuquerque taproom is near the trendy district of Nob Hill, it, like the brewery's original home (in a semirural part of Los Lunas), has a tractor parked in front. *Courtesy the author.*

style had become very popular in New Mexico, and you couldn't do without one." More recently, #15 Pilsner, a German-style lager, has been added to the regular list. "We called it #15 because we use fifteen bags of pale malt for each batch, we first brewed it on the fifteenth of the month and it was our fifteenth brew of the year. At the taproom, they also call it Minnesota Moline Pilsner."

Soon the beer farm was again thriving. Expansion to Albuquerque, where the craft beer market was growing at an incredible speed, seemed the logical next step. In the summer of 2011, Tractor opened a taproom in Albuquerque's trendy Nob Hill district. Located in a building that used to be home to a bookstore and then a Pilates studio and a spinning shop (where people rode stationary bikes), it became an almost instant success. "Soon," Hargis remarked, "we were just able to keep up with the demand, both in Los Lunas and Albuquerque."

"Opening the taproom gave us a second chance," Hargis said. "It gave us a wonderful outlet for our beer." Production increased dramatically, and the brew house was expanded. Then, in 2013, one of the administrators at Premier Distributing, the largest beer distributor in New Mexico, approached Hargis and Devore about the possibility of Tractor's resuming bottling of its beer. "He was a regular at the Nob Hill taproom, and he liked our beer,"

Hargis remembered. "He told us that Premier wanted a local product for the liquor and beer outlets they serviced."

Hargis and Devore, who would soon be named employee-owners of the company, agreed. They began by rebranding the product, replacing the cartoon-like labels for Farmer's Tan Red Ale and Farmer's Almanac IPA with new stylized logos. Now that both the red ale and the IPA would be available in bottles around the state, it became imperative that the old brew house, which was operating at capacity, be expanded or replaced. The decision was made to close down operations in Los Lunas and open a combined brewery and taproom/restaurant just north of downtown Albuquerque. Production from the fifteen-barrel system would be increased as there would now be nine thirty-barrel and five fifteen-barrel fermenters. The new system began operating at the beginning of 2014.

In describing Tractor's five regular beers, Hargis noted that he worked to create clean, enjoyable beers that were somewhere in the middle range in terms of hoppiness and alcohol content. "If I have twelve beers on tap," he said, "I want at least six to be in the middle range. I don't want to overwhelm people." Farmer's Tan, at 6.5 percent ABV one of Tractor's stronger brews, is a hybrid of Irish red and Scotch ale styles. A dark bronze in color and medium-bodied, it is a smooth ale in which the malts dominate. Haymaker Honey Wheat, which he describes as an excellent introduction for newcomers to craft beer, uses eighty pounds of local honey in each fifteen-barrel brew. Although it is an American wheat ale, it resembles a hefeweizen and is "something our German visitors really enjoy."

Double Plowed Oatmeal Stout is a dry, English-style drink that uses chocolate and dark roasted malts. At 5.2 percent ABV, it is a very popular beer among the regulars at the Nob Hill taproom. Sod Buster is categorized as an American-style pale ale. An easy-to-drink beer that resembles its English counterpart, it balances hop and malt notes. Although its International Bitterness Units rating is 45, the hops don't overwhelm. Farmer's Almanac IPA, at 72 IBUs, is the closest Hargis comes to brewing a hop bomb. Golden in color, the hops contribute citrus notes as well as bitterness. This very popular ale has an alcohol content of 6.25 percent ABV. He notes that it is more of an East Coast style, not as citrusy as a West Coast IPA. "We are gradually changing it to a more West Coast style as the appropriate hops become available."

For a small business that nearly "bought the farm" a few years ago, Tractor Brewing is now thriving. The main difference is that Tractor is now an urban "beer farm."

CHAPTER 3
ALBUQUERQUE, EAST OF INTERSTATE 25

IL VICINO BREWING COMPANY

2381 Aztec Road NE, Albuquerque, 87107
505-881-2737, www.ilvicino.com
Taproom: At the brewery. Beers are also available at Il Vicino restaurants: 3403 Central
Avenue NE, Albuquerque; 11225 Montgomery Boulevard NE, Albuquerque; 10701
Coralles Boulevard NW, Albuquerque; and 321 West San Francisco Street, Santa Fe.

In 1993, Tom Hennessy, one of the owners of the Il Vicino restaurant, located in Albuquerque's Nob Hill shopping area, decided that the trattoria-style establishment, which specialized in thin-crust Italian pizza baked in wood-fired ovens, should brew its own beer. A casual home-brewer, he was aware of the growing popularity of brewpubs and reasoned that, given Il Vicino patrons' enthusiasm for the microbrewed Celis wheat beer that Il Vicino "imported" from Texas, good brews made on the premises would be even more popular.

Hennessy and his newly hired brewer Rob Chavez cobbled together a three-barrel brewing system out of old brewing tanks from England and assorted dairy equipment, removed the dishwashers from a ten- by ten-foot space at the back of the restaurant and began to create their own beer. In

1994, Il Vicino offered its first beer, Old Route 66 Golden Ale, to thirsty patrons, who responded enthusiastically. Soon after, the restaurant began to offer the style that was extremely popular on the West Coast: India pale ale.

Chavez died in a tragic motorcycle accident in 1995, and Brady McKeown, who has been with Il Vicino ever since, assumed brewing duties. "I was studying at the university and working part time at the restaurant. I'd been an American pale lager drinker, the usual stuff, but I really liked the Celis beers they served. I started to hang around Rob Chavez and really became interested in what he was doing, and he made me his assistant. When Il Vicino started opening locations in Colorado, I set up the brewing operations there. Then I returned to Albuquerque." In 1996, the young and relatively inexperienced brewer's brown ale won a silver medal at the Great American Beer Festival. Since then, he and members of his brewing team have won a gold medal, three silver and three bronze at the GABF.

It didn't take long for the cramped brewery to become inadequate to satisfy the growing enthusiasm of Albuquerque's beer drinkers, and brewing operations were moved to another building. Then, with the brewery having to supply two new restaurants in Albuquerque and one in Santa Fe, a second move became necessary. In 2011, a new seven-barrel brew house, along with a tap-room/canteen, was opened.

With the opening of the new facility, Il Vicino joined a growing number of taprooms in Albuquerque where patrons could enjoy not only a brewery's regular offerings but also trial brews and one-offs. These included small batches fermented in casks and barrel-aged beers. There is a small kitchen, right behind the bar, where "noshes" such as a beer sponge pretzel and "Swanky" sandwiches such as a brewer's brat and a knuckle sandwich (prosciutto, salami, mozzarella cheese, arugula and roasted red peppers) are prepared. In addition, patrons can sit either inside or on the outside covered patio, enjoying the frequent live music presentations.

David Facey, manager of the taproom/restaurant, which is known as I.B.C. Canteen, explained that

> the old brewery was producing beer for the restaurants. Here we decided to capitalize on the growing taproom phenomenon. People enjoy drinking beer where it's made. In the restaurants, the draw is the food, with beer available as a beverage. Here it's the exact opposite: people come for the beer and enjoy the food and music. And our patrons aren't just beer geeks; we get the after-work crowd dropping by, cyclists who've been on the North Canal Trail [just two blocks away] and, on Sundays, families. And they get a

In addition to brewing for the company's restaurants in Albuquerque and Santa Fe, the Il Vicino Brewery is also the site of a taproom, the Canteen, which serves specialty beers and regularly presents local musicians. *Courtesy the author.*

chance to meet our brewers—Brady, Doug Cochran and Zach Guilmette.
They often come out from the back to talk to the customers.

The most popular of Il Vicino's six regular beers is Wet Mountain IPA, which accounts for more than 50 percent of the brewery's sales. One of the first IPAs to be brewed in New Mexico, this 7.2 percent ABV, 80 IBU beverage is much hoppier than the first version created by Tom Hennessy in 1995. "It wasn't until I spent time in Colorado that I really understood what an IPA could be," Brady McKeown explained. "Now it's got a lot more hops, and there are a lot more varieties of hops that we can include in the brew." In 2010, 2011 and 2012, Wet Mountain or its variations have won the annual New Mexico IPA Challenge, no mean feat in a state that has many award-winning IPAs.

While Wet Mountain IPA may be Il Vicino's best-selling beer, an almost completely different beer is its most decorated. Slow Down Brown Ale, a 6.4 percent ABV, 35 IBU malt-forward beer, was partly inspired by Pete's Wicked Ale, a popular 1990s microbrew from the West Coast. "We didn't want our beer to be as malty or sweet as Pete's," Brady noted. "We wanted it more in the American brown style, but not too hop-forward." He combined English malts with West Coast hops to provide the desired balance. Slow Down Brown won a gold medal at the World Beer Cup of 1996 and, since then, has won a combined total of one gold, one silver and three bronzes at the World Beer Cup and Great American Beer Festival.

Il Vicino offers four other beers on a year-round basis, two light and two dark. Pigtail Pilsner is a 5.4 percent ABV German pilsner, which uses pilsner malt and Saaz and Hallertau hops and achieves a less malty, more bitter flavor than its Czech counterpart. It is filtered to give it a clarity similar to European pilsners. 28 M is an American wheat ale that uses 25 percent wheat malt. At 4.0 percent ABV and 12 IBUs, this is the brewery's lightest offering.

Dark & Lusty Stout includes pale and caramel malts and roasted unmalted barley to achieve a flavor not unlike Guinness's renowned version of the style. At 8.0 percent ABV, it is a strong beer; 60 IBUs work to balance the sweetness of the malts. The simply named Amber (6.1 percent ABV and 40 IBUs) is a fairly standard rendition of a popular American style. The stout and amber are available year round only at the Canteen.

The opening of the Canteen and the subsequent attraction of a large contingent of knowledgeable beer drinkers provided Brady and his bunch with the opportunity to brew some lesser-known seasonals and one-offs. "Fruit beers have been very popular," McKeown noted. These include blueberry-, raspberry-, boysenberry- and even kiwi-flavored brews. "We once did an apricot-flavored saison." In 2012, the Chocolate Cherry Milk Stout won a bronze medal at the Great American Beer Festival, and in 2013, Panama Joe Stout took home the gold in the Coffee Beer category. The most unusual one-off was a Christmas offering called Fruitcake. Brady smiled as he described the unusual combination of ingredients. "It was a strong ale [9 percent ABV], and we used fruit, molasses and cinnamon; later we added cranberry, tart cherries and orange and lemon zest. Even people who said they hated fruitcake loved it."

A recent one-off brew was called Just Esteem, a California common beer that had frequently been called "California steam beer" until Anchor Brewing of San Francisco copyrighted the name in the 1970s. Il Vicino's nickname, with its tongue-in-cheek reference to the copyrighted term, provides people with a hint of what it might taste like and expresses the mild annoyance that many brewers and beer aficionados have felt about Anchor's legal expropriation of the term. The Canteen also serves cask- and barrel-conditioned ales. The former are very small batches that are fermented in casks, where they produce carbon dioxide naturally. Barrel-aged beers are left to mature in wine or bourbon oak barrels and acquire notes of the flavors of the previous "occupants." Recent barrel-aged beers have included a Belgian golden strong ale and a Belgian golden dark strong.

"Believe in beer." That's the motto at Il Vicino. And it's one that the Brady (McKeown) Bunch subscribes to. Brewing is hard work, and it doesn't make them rich. But day by day, the positive responses of imbibers at the Canteen and Il Vicino restaurants around the state indicate that Brady's patrons are believers as well.

KELLYS BREW PUB

3222 Central Avenue SE, Albuquerque, 87106
505-262-2739, www.kellysbrewpub.com
Taproom: At the brewery.

On the southwest corner of Central Avenue and Wellesley Drive, just a few blocks east of the main campus of the University of New Mexico, a large circular sign highlighted by a red star, the letter *K* within, is mounted at the

Kellys is located in a historic Albuquerque building that originally contained a Texaco station and Albuquerque's first Ford dealership. *Courtesy the author.*

top of a very tall pole. Across the top point of the star is printed the word "Kellys." To the sides are the words "Food" and "Pub" and at the bottom the word "Brew." At the top of the wall of the building behind the sign, the word "Food" is repeated.

Since April 2000, the building has been the home of Kellys Brew Pub, Albuquerque's second-oldest such establishment. In warm and hot weather, patrons sit beneath umbrellas at tables on the patio that stretches along the west and north sides of the building. Those who prefer a great deal of shade can walk through the large roll-back doors that lead to the bar and restaurant.

Anyone who passed by Kellys when the brewpub wasn't open or when cold weather forced the closing of a patio could be excused if they thought they were passing a service station and automobile dealership. The mounted sign resembles the ones that used to identify Texaco stations, and the style of the lettering on the face of the building is the same as that once used at Ford dealerships. In fact, when the building opened in 1939, it housed Jones Motor Company, the first Ford dealership in the area, and a Texaco station. The sliding doors that now lead into the bar area used to open into the service bays; those leading into the restaurant opened into the showroom. The two small doors through which waiters now pass, bringing food to the patio, once led into the customers' washrooms. In the short hallways behind these doors are paintings of a man and a woman washing their hands.

Kellys was founded in 1996 by Dennis Bonfantine, a veteran of many years in the liquor business. In his student days at Whittier College in California, he had worked part time delivering beer for a local distributor. After graduation, he became the New Mexico and west Texas sales representative for Olympia Brewery of Washington State, and then he went on to run New Mexico Beverage Company, Vintage Wines and Spirits and Kellys Discount Liquor Stores (which he sold in 2000).

"Over the years, I became aware of the growing craft beer movement on the West Coast, and then, as a liquor store owner, I came into contact with the Colorado microbrewing scene. Around the same time, I learned about the Brew Your Own Beer business and visited some of these companies in California, Arizona and Colorado," Bonfantine recalled. "Starting a business where people could brew beer under our supervision and in our building seemed like a good way to go."

When he learned that in New Mexico a Brew Your Own Beer establishment had to have a brewer's license, he decided that he might as well brew and sell his own beer. "And," he added, "if I had beer, I would need food. So I found someone to run a kitchen." Kellys opened in 1996 just west of the location it now occupies. The brewpub quickly became a popular spot. But in 1999, the owners of the building wouldn't renew Bonfantine's lease. The Jones building, just down the street, was the only vacant and nearby place that had the room for a brewpub with a growing clientele.

The Ford dealership and Texaco station had long since moved, and after housing other tenants, the building had fallen into disrepair and suffered from the attacks of vandals—even though it was on the National Register of Historic Places and the New Mexico Register of Cultural Properties. "Officials wanted to make sure that we kept the historic nature of the place intact," Bonfantine remembered. "We reconstructed the original Art Moderne style of the exterior of the building. Then we added the sign and the lettering, advertising what we are and reminding people of what the building used to be."

After Kellys relocated to the Jones building, it became even more successful. "We were swamped as soon as we opened. People were drinking our beer as fast as we could make it, so we had to bring in some other people's craft beers and contracted some of our brewing out. Now we've expanded our own brewery so that we don't have to be so dependent on outside brewers."

Kellys head brewer Dan Cavin stands in front of a mural depicting the steps in brewing from grain to glass. *Courtesy the author.*

Since its inception, Kellys has had a large beer list—three six-packs of styles are generally available. "Because we started as a 'brew your own,' we had a lot of small kettles," Bonfantine explained. "So we could create small batches of many different styles. If one turned out badly, we could pour it out and not lose much money. And if one were off-style, we could sell it as a 'Brewer's Special.'" The eighteen beers on the menu range from the 4.9 percent ABV blonde ale to an 8 percent ABV imperial stout. Several of the brews are under 5 percent ABV and are designed as gateway or crossover beers that can lead drinkers used to mainstream lagers into the craft beer world. What began as blonde ale has been turned into a lager that uses corn in addition to malted barley to make the flavor more familiar to drinkers of national brands. Two of the most popular beers are India pale ale (which is a hearty 6.3 percent ABV beer), and Weizen, which is the top summer seller. There are also such lesser-known styles as alt bier, dunkelweizen and black bitter.

Head Brewer Dan Cavin, who also oversees the Brew Your Own Beer operations, joined Kellys soon after the move to the new building. An Albuquerque native who brewed his own beer, he had been sitting at Il Vicino, across and down the street from Kellys, having a drink with the current Kellys brewer, who told him that he needed someone to help one day a week and asked if Cavin would be interested. Dan was, went to work the next week and, a year later, became head brewer. He left to brew in Colorado for a few years and returned to Kellys in 2006.

"Very early in my career," he said, "I learned my most important brewing lesson: KISS—Keep It Simple Stupid." He began by following the basic style guidelines and has gradually tinkered with recipes to create beers that possess a characteristic that, he said, most appeals to Kellys' customers. "And they are becoming more sophisticated each year. Ever since Chama River and Marble started creating their IPAs, people have wanted beers that are hoppier. So I've been toning down the malt profile of some of the ales."

Kellys has standard but good pub-style food, and this being New Mexico, many of the dishes feature green chile. The beers neither threaten nor overwhelm, but they do offer the large number of people who flock to the brewpub introductions to a variety of styles they might never have heard of or, until the last decade, have wanted to taste.

Six decades ago, motorists along Central Avenue turned in at the Texaco star for quality cars and good service. Today, they still turn in at the Kellys star for quality and good service. The quality they look for is not in automobiles, though, but in beer and food.

LA CUMBRE BREWING COMPANY

3313 Girard Boulevard NE, Albuquerque, 87107
505-872-0225, www.lacumbrewing.com
Taproom: At the brewery.

Jeff Erway, owner and the first brewer of Albuquerque's La Cumbre Brewing Company, grew up in Rochester, New York, a place he described as the "capital of industrial beer." Home of Genesee Cream Ale, a beverage pleasing to aging drinkers whose palates have been enhanced by clouds of nostalgia, it was also home to the "World of Beers," an enormous store that stocked both craft and European beers. "I really hated the stuff we used to sneak out of parents' fridges when we were in high school," he remembered. "But then I discovered that beer could taste really good and that there were a lot of very good beers, like Newcastle Brown and Samuel Smith's Ale."

It was his discovery of Sierra Nevada Pale Ale that led to his becoming a professional brewer. "Laura [his then fiancée] and I had gone to Church Rock in the Navajo Nation, where I was hired to teach music," Erway explained. "We were a long way away from any store that stocked Sierra Nevada Pale Ale. One day, I discovered a book on home-brewing and decided that if I couldn't find good beer readily available, I would try to make some myself." Pretty soon, his beers started winning awards, and the home-brewer-by-necessity attracted the attention of Ted Rice, brewmaster at Albuquerque's Chama River. "He told me that with professional training, I could find work as a brewer." Jeff enrolled in the American Brewers Guild in Vermont, with some of his training taking place at Chama River under Rice's guidance. In 2005, Erway began working at Chama River with his mentor Rice. When Rice moved on in 2007 to found Marble Brewery, Jeff became the head brewer. Two of his recipes won bronze medals at the Great American Beer Festival: Zwickel in 2008 and Three Dog Stout in 2010.

Although working at what he loved, Erway wanted to own his own microbrewery. "Every brewer dreams of being given carte blanche, of pushing the envelope, putting his own stamp on what he creates," he explained. With moral and financial encouragement from friends and relatives, he made the big step. La Cumbre opened in December 2010. The name, from the Spanish for mountain peak, reflects his love of the mountainous outdoors of New Mexico and emphasizes, as one of the company's slogans states, the aim of presenting "New Mexico beers at their peak."

Jeff wanted to open his new business with a big beer, an IPA that, in his words, "would knock your socks off. I had tasted so many uncompelling IPAs; I wanted one that was well-executed and righteously hoppy." The result was Elevated IPA, which weighs in at a strong 7.2 percent ABV and a bitterness rating of 100 IBUs. "It was the most intensely hoppy beer I could make: it had bitterness and a variety of hop aromas and flavors."

La Cumbre quickly became a success. Within the first year, Erway increased brewing capacity, and in 2012, the second full year of operation, production doubled to nearly 3,100 barrels. Enthusiasts flocked to the taproom. They sat around tables that Erway had made from old wine barrels, looked at the shelves decorated with the hundreds of beer bottles from his collection, thoughtfully obeyed the sign posted near the taps announcing a three-beer limit, chatted, read newspapers and, on special evenings, listened to live music. Dogs, on leashes only, often sat beside their owners, watching the activities. Outside the crowded taproom, food trucks provided eats for the imbibers inside.

In 2011, with the brewery less than ten months old, La Cumbre received national recognition. Elevated IPA garnered the gold medal at the Great American Beer Festival, beating out more than two hundred other entries in the American-style IPA category. The simply named BEER earned a gold in the American and International Style Pilsner category, while Malpais Stout earned a silver in the Foreign Stout category.

By early 2012, it had become obvious that La Cumbre needed not only more brewing equipment but also a new head brewer, someone with extensive experience who could free up Jeff to concentrate more on the business side of operations. He chose Daniel Jaramillo, who'd been working in the industry since 1992. "I'd never home-brewed," Jaramillo explained. "I started doing Joe jobs at Rio Bravo [a defunct brewery] in Albuquerque, but when the assistant brewer quit, I took over his position. I never had any formal training; I learned everything I know on the job." Daniel spent time at Albuquerque's short-lived Bavarian Lager Cellar and Assets Bar and Grill before working for Blue Corn in Santa Fe and then Marble back in Albuquerque.

Speaking of his new head brewer, Erway praises not only Jaramillo's wide-ranging experience but also his skills as a lager brewer. "Sometimes the palate can get burned out by very hoppy beers, and a well-brewed lager provides an excellent alternative," Jeff explained. "Lagers are returning to popularity, but they are very difficult to brew well, and Daniel does one of the best jobs that I know." Jaramillo's talents are well displayed in South Peak Pilsner, a light-bodied Bohemian-style lager that is given crispness from the

Czech Saaz hops and a mild malt background from the continental pilsner malts. The 4.8 percent ABV beverage is brewed to be true to the European style and, Erway emphatically noted, "is not designed for the Bud drinker." La Cumbre's other lagers include No, You're a Dort, in the style of northern German Dortmunder Export lager, and Where in the Helles, a Munich-style lager. For those who wanted something like the ubiquitous mass-produced light beers but with some flavor, La Cumbre has offered the generically named BEER, an American-style Pilsner.

In addition to Elevated IPA and South Peak Pilsner, there are three other year-round La Cumbre beers. A Slice of Hefen, is a Bavarian-style hefeweizen. It's a 5.4 percent ABV brew with only 15 IBUs, one of the brewery's least hoppy offerings. Rich and yet clean finishing, the beer's flavor is enhanced with notes of clove, banana and vanilla. Pyramid Rock Pale Ale (5.8 percent ABV, 55 IBUs) was designed to reflect English versions of the style. English hops and English crystal malts provide earthy notes not found in American versions. "It's very similar to an English ESB; the hoppy elements are more than balanced by the malts," Erway noted. Malpais Stout is a hefty 7.0 percent ABV. "It's rich and chewy, but the hops give it a bitterness not found in English or Irish stouts."

Erway and Jaramillo have also brewed several one-offs and seasonal beers. Twelve of these are definitely "big beers," with ABVs of 7 percent or above. Four have been in double figures. Eight have been IPAs or pale ales, three have been stouts or porters and there have been two Belgian-style ales. Asked to name his most unusual beer, Erway quickly replied, "Café Con Leche, a combination of coffee and milk stout; we used twenty pounds of coffee in each batch." The most unusual name? Three Legged Dog, an 11 percent imperial IPA, brewed in aid of an animal humane charity.

In conversations, both Jeff Erway and Dan Jaramillo frequently use the world "palate." That, they say, is because a well-developed, discriminating palate is essential if a brewer is to achieve the goals he has set for each style he brews. For Jeff, palate development began as soon as he made his first purchases at Rochester's "World of Beer." Initially, it was a matter of distinguishing between what was good and what was bad; later, it became an awareness of what was good and what was *better*, as well as why. When he became a brewer, how to achieve the taste results that he desired became important. "When you know why a beer tastes the way it does and that it doesn't taste the way you want it to," Erway explained, "you ask yourself, 'How did this happen?'" Jaramillo added, "What stands out in the malts and hops? What are the flaws? What can I do to make it better? Good beer calls you back for another. How do you make a beer that does that? You strive to make all your beers encourage customers to come back for another."

Judging by the responses to La Cumbre during its first three years of operation, Jeff and Daniel have been doing that with amazing consistency.

NEXUS BREWERY AND RESTAURANT

4730 Pan American Freeway, Albuquerque, 87109
505-242-4100, www.nexusbrewery.com
Taproom: At the brewery.

Late in the 1990s, New Mexico banker Ken Carson began a hobby that would change the course of his professional life. "I'd heard that Kellys restaurant was offering a program for people to brew their own beer. I didn't know much about beer at the time—just Miller and Coors. If I wanted something special, I'd order a Mexican beer."

The first beer Carson created was a Scottish ale. "It was quite an experience. I really liked the big malty flavors. I made other beers, and whenever I'd travel on business, I'd try out the local beers. It was wonderful to discover the tremendous variety of styles." He would also visit restaurants that specialized in his two favorite kinds of meals: soul food and New Mexican.

During the first decade of the twenty-first century, Carson continued his successful career in banking, as a New Mexico State banking commissioner and then as president of My Bank in Belen, a half hour's drive south of Albuquerque. When he wasn't being practical, he'd occasionally allow himself to dream. Wouldn't it be wonderful to open a restaurant that brewed its own beer and served soul food and New Mexican? As the craft brewing movement grew in Albuquerque, he began to see that there could be room for another brewpub...if it offered something different. "It would not be a place that brewed the really hoppy beers that so many of the new places featured, and its food would be what I called 'New Mexico soul.'"

In addition to liking malty beers and New Mexican soul food, Carson was an avid fan of *Star Trek*. And so, when he decided to start his own brewpub, he decided that it would be a "Nexus"—a place, as all "Trekkies" know, where everything is perfect. It would also be a meeting point, a literal nexus, where people could gather to enjoy one another's company over a beer and a meal.

In creating his nexus, Carson sought the advice of Dr. Paul Farnsworth, a chemist with a specialization in fermentation who had worked as a consultant with many breweries and who, at the time, was teaching at the University of New Mexico. "He told me, 'You need to do *you* in your beer and menus.' Of course, that was soul and New Mexican and malty."

He interviewed Manuel Mussen, the person who became Nexus's head brewer, via Skype. A recent graduate of the brewing program at the University of California–Davis, Mussen was a young "veteran" in the making of beer. He'd been a home-brewer during his high school years in the small southern California town of Julian and had worked, "usually without pay," doing various jobs at Rock Bottom and AleSmith, two brewpubs in the San Diego area. "I learned most of the important practical things a brewer needs to know working in San Diego. At Davis, I got the theoretical background you can't do without." After graduation, he headed to England for the summer, serving as a kind of postgraduate intern at St. Austell, a 150-year-old brewery in Cornwall, England. "I was only there for a few months, but they taught me how to really make English ales."

Before May 2011, Carson, Farnsworth (who had stayed on as the "master brewer" and chief consultant) and Mussen worked to put together the brew house, develop beer recipes and create a menu. The equipment for the brew house came from Assets Grill, Albuquerque's first brewpub, which had ceased operations in 2005. "I don't know if it had been used since then," Mussen remembered. "But it sure was dirty; there was old beer in the bottom of some of the tanks." The beer menu would emphasize malty beer, relatively low in hop profiles. There would be beers that would appeal to craft brew novices, along with a Scottish ale, Carson's favorite style. In fact, as Mussen explained, "The beers reflected the owner's preferences. They were dark, malty—something different from what the other breweries in the area were doing."

Speaking of the restaurant, Carson remarked, "At first we envisioned ourselves as a brewery that also made food. We planned a very small menu— paninis and snacks that could be made in a small area behind the bar. But then we decided to offer a bigger menu with full luncheon and dinner plates. Over our first two years, the situation has reversed: we are now a restaurant that makes its own beer. We've enlarged our kitchen and increased our staff."

A glance at the menu reveals the nature of the oxymoronically named restaurant style, "New Mexico soul food." On the one hand, there are red or green chile nachos, pico de gallo (salsa) and home-style open-face enchiladas. On the other hand, there is southern fried chicken and waffles, southern fried fish sliders (with a freshwater fish said to be better than catfish), collard greens and New Orleans–style gumbo.

Manuel Mussen has created a variety of offerings from light to dark and from medium strength to very strong. White Ale was designed to capitalize on the popularity of Blue Moon Belgian White, a product of the brewing giant Coors. At 5.7 percent ABV, Nexus's version was moderately strong but had only 14 IBUs, making it gentle enough to guide novices into the craft beer scene. "We add coriander and orange spices, but it's not as spicy as most Belgian whites," Mussen explained. Cream Ale, the other lighter brew designed as an entry-level beer, has an interesting history. "It uses corn and was one of the more frequently brewed styles in earlier New England times, where corn was easier to get than barley." Nexus's 5.0 percent ABV, 10 IBU version of the style was created for people who might want to order what the taproom definitely doesn't serve: Bud Light. A mix of corn, malted wheat and U.S. pilsner malt provides the beer's light body and smooth texture.

Nexus also brews an IPA and a red ale in the American style. The red ale, 6.2 percent ABV and 45 IBUs, uses caramel malts and emphasizes hops, although, Mussen added, "our red isn't as hoppy as some of the others you'll find in Albuquerque. Our IPA is kind of West Coast...I dial back on the hoppiness. One of the problems is that we are limited by the variety of hops we can get. One of the best available is Falconer's Flight, which is a blend of several hops and gives citrusy, piney notes."

Nexus's stout, one of the two regular dark offerings, is in the English style. "We've worked at getting it roastier and darker; we don't make it as hoppy as some American versions of the style." At 4.9 percent ABV and 30 IBUs, it is a good session beer. The Scottish ale, Ken Carson's favorite and Nexus's flagship beer, is a very malt-forward beer, dark brown, with nutty and toffee flavors. "Scottish yeasts give it a smoky flavor," Mussen explained, adding, "It's not hoppy because Scottish beers generally aren't that hoppy; in the old days, they didn't have easy access to hops." It is smooth-bodied with a clean finish. It weighs in at a strong 7.0 percent ABV but has only 28 IBUs.

Mussen has brewed several seasonal and one-off beers, including a brown, an ESB, a California common and a Belgian tripel. The two of which he is most proud are imperial versions of the cream and Scottish ales. The imperial Scottish ale's nickname, "Beam Me Up Scotty," is a reminder not only of Carson's love of *Star Trek* but also that, at 10.7 percent ABV, it is in no way a session beer. The Imperial Cream Ale, 9.5 percent ABV, earned a silver medal in the Other Strong Beer category at the 2012 World Beer Cup competition. It has the smoothness and mellow taste of the regular cream ale, but it is certainly, to use one of the brewery's advertising words, a real "exBEERience."

Although pleased with their successes during the first two and a half years that Nexus has been, as it declares, "Albuquerque's Craft Beer & Soul Food Connection," Carson, Mussen and the restaurant staff have been working to strengthen the nexus. Their goal is to make a stronger connection with Albuquerque's growing and increasingly knowledgeable craft beer aficionados.

SANDIA CHILE GRILL & BREWERY

7120 Wyoming Boulevard NE, #7D, Albuquerque, 87109
505-798-1970, www.sandiachilegrill.com
Taproom: At the brewery.

Since 2003, Mick Coker, along with Clinton, his son, has been serving what many consider some of the best New Mexican food in Albuquerque. Coker started Sandia Chile Grill because, he said, "I felt there was a niche for this kind of restaurant." The menu features burritos, enchiladas and tacos, all of which are made fresh on the grill behind the walk-up counter. "But," Mick remembered, "we lacked one thing that would make it a destination for more people: beer. One day, a relative jokingly remarked that we should make vodka from the water in which we boiled all the potatoes we used every day."

That got Mick and Clinton thinking. "We certainly weren't going to make vodka," said Clinton, who spent time at Central New Mexico College studying culinary arts. He and his dad talked over the possibility of brewing beer. It could be made right on the premises, just like the food. Some of the equipment they already had could be used to make beer, and "we would be serving better and less expensive beer than if we just ordered products from the megabrewers."

Neither Mick nor Clinton was a stranger to the art of making alcoholic beverages. The two had long been interested in creating ciders and meads, and their amateur efforts reached fruition in 2011 when their Hard Apple Cider was named the "Best of Show" in the New Mexico Pro-Amateur competition.

Mick and Clinton Coker are the father-and-son brewing team at Sandia Chile Grill & Brewery. *Courtesy the author.*

They did not rush into making beer available at their restaurant but rather took two years developing an amber ale. "We spent a little time day by day, learning the processes, tweaking our recipe to make each batch better," Mick remembered. "Whenever I'd wake up in the middle of the night, I'd lie there thinking about what we'd been doing and about how I could make some adjustments the next day." When they began to serve their beer on July 1, 2012, Mick and Clinton offered a honey wheat ale, an India pale ale and Smoked Milk Stout.

Speaking of their core offerings, Clinton, who is in charge of brewing, remarked, "We want to make beers with flavors that will appeal to both the novice and the experienced beer drinker." Honey Wheat Ale has banana notes and uses honey from the Sonoran Desert. Smooth Move Amber Ale's pale and caramel malts are balanced with five hop varieties that give it a zesty finish. Sun Ranger Irish Red Ale, which is not as highly hopped as the American version of the style, emphasizes the pale, caramel and roasted malts. Rattlesnake IPA has an International Bitterness Unit count of 88, somewhat less than most other Albuquerque IPAs. "I think we'll be upping the hop content a little," Mick suggested. Their entry on the dark side is Smoked Milk Stout, brewed with cherry wood smoked malts.

"We'll be having some seasonal beers, as well as these five," Clinton noted. "Right now, we have a Double Pilsner. It's 8 percent alcohol by volume. It's been quite popular." Then, after a thoughtful pause, he added, "except with the Bud and Corona drinkers."

Visitors entering Sandia Chile Grill & Brewery will notice two fairly large vessels along the wall between the front door and the kitchen area. One of these serves as a hot liquor tank and kettle and the other as the mash tun for the 1.6-barrel brewing system. The fermenters and the conditioning tanks are in the back. "It's not big, and it's simple," Mick said, "but it's the end product that's important."

An open laptop is on one of the tables at the back of the restaurant. "That's my office," Mick said, chuckling. Judging from early response to their brews and the ongoing appreciation of the food, Mick may soon have to vacate his "office" to make room for the growing number of customers.

CHAPTER 4

ALBUQUERQUE, BEYOND THE CITY LIMITS

KAKTUS BREWING COMPANY

471 South Hill Road, Bernalillo, 87004
505-379-5072, www.kaktusbrewery.com
Taproom: At the brewery.

The idea to open a brewpub in Bernalillo, which had been without one since Milagro Brewery closed in 2005, was born while Dana Koller's family was sitting in the backyard, enjoying beer from a keg provided by Mark Matheson, a family friend and the brewer at Turtle Mountain Brewing Company in Rio Rancho. "People were talking about interesting projects that they'd like to undertake," Koller remembered, "when somebody mentioned that there was no brewpub in Bernalillo and said that something should be done about that."

It wasn't long before the suggestion became a firm idea. Dana's father, John, owned suitable property near Interstate 25, next to a KOA campground, and an eight-minute walk from the Bernalillo Rail Runner Station. Dana, who had been introduced to craft beer by his father and had become a "beer enthusiast," had a degree in hospitality management and marketing from the University of New Mexico. Matheson, who offered

Dana Koller stands beside the desert plants that give Kaktus Brewing Company in Bernalillo its name. *Courtesy the author.*

to help wherever he could, had the expertise in setting up breweries, developing recipes and making beer.

Dana didn't want to create a brewery that was just the same as the more than a dozen places found in Albuquerque and neighboring towns. Those made award-winning IPAs and bracing imperial stouts and porters, but he felt that "beer drinkers would soon be looking for something that wasn't really hoppy or really strong. I felt that the future would include a lot more beers that were maltier in flavor and lower in alcohol. That's why I decided we'd focus on German-style lagers."

He also wanted the brewery to be part of the community, both socially and environmentally. He would focus on making his planned brewpub a destination where people from the area could come, bring their children, have some beer and food and enjoy one another's company. He also wanted to create a sustainable brewery, one that recycled its water, composted its waste and generated as much solar power as possible. And so, Kaktus Brewing Company (named from the German word for cactus) was created, the name itself symbolic of both the type of beers it would create and a prominent feature of the landscape.

It's a little difficult to spot the brewpub driving down South Hill Road, which seems like a typical less-traveled, New Mexico country road. A small sign with the brewery name and a figure of a kokopelli carrying a pint glass of beer instead of a flute is nearly hidden by cholla cactuses. The gravel drive that slopes down to the parking lot and patio is bordered first by solar panels and then by old doors and window frames brightly repainted, discarded objects reclaimed and repurposed. The building is a two-car garage expanded by 1,200 square feet to include the taproom, a small kitchen and a brew house, with a brand-new German-built two-barrel system. There are two patios— one in front with a wood-burning fireplace and the other in the back with games for children and adults to play. At the edge of the property, near a wide dirt trail that heads toward the Rail Runner stop, there is a hitching post. "We've had a couple of people arrive on horseback," Dana explained.

The lighter but flavorful beers created by Mike Waddy, a former home-brewer who had been mentored by Mike Matheson, include three English (an ESB, a pale ale and a porter) and two German styles (a helles and a hefeweizen). Of these, the strongest beer is the ESB, at 5 percent ABV. The porter is 4.8 percent ABV and relatively light-bodied. "It tastes like porter," Koller noted, "but you won't feel like you've had a meal after you've enjoyed a glass." The helles, a maltier German lager, was 4.3 percent ABV, and the hefe was 4.2. "We have plans for a dunkelweizen, which isn't often brewed in this area, and other German beers. We'll have a rotating list. And we're tweaking our recipes, working to get them just where we want them."

The object, Koller emphasized, is for patrons to enjoy the flavor of the beer as they enjoy one another's company. They can have two or maybe even three and still safely drive (or ride their horses) home. People staying at the KOA next door can walk, not stumble, back to their trailers and campers.

LAS CAZUELA'S MEXICAN GRILL & BREWERY

4051 Sara Road SE, Rio Rancho, 87124
505-994-9364, www.cazuelasmexicangrill.com
Taproom: At the brewery.

During the first decade of the twenty-first century, Las Cazuela's Mexican Grill (the name comes from the word for cooking pot) served standard Mexican and

American beers, including such familiar brands as Corona, Tecate, Bud Light and Coors. Then, just as Albuquerque's Il Vicino and Santa Fe's Blue Corn had in the 1990s, the restaurant installed its own brew house.

"People weren't going to go out of their way to search for another Mexican restaurant," manager Jude Sanchez explained. "But they would look for a microbrewery." At the time, there was only one brewpub in Rio Rancho, Turtle Mountain, and the market was certainly able to support and ready for another. The restaurant, which began brewing and selling its own beer in 2013, was just across Sara Road from the city's largest employer, Intel. Beer brewed on premises would be a great attraction for thirsty workers after they finished their shifts. In fact, to cater to Intel personnel working on night shifts, Las Cazuela's introduced a Wednesday morning brunch. "We wanted to give them a 'happy hour' like people on the day shift enjoyed," Jude laughed.

A banquet room behind the bar area became a seven-barrel brew house, and Mike Campbell, who had discovered what good beer was while serving in the army in Germany and who had been the first brewer at Tractor Brewing in Los Lunas, was hired to make the beer. "They pretty much gave me carte blanche," he remarked, "although they wanted me to have at least two beers that would please customers who had been used to Mexican lagers. They wanted the beers to be relatively simple and to have drinkability."

Acapulco Gold, a 5.2 percent ABV lager and the first Mexican lager Campbell had ever brewed, is, he noted, "a Bohemian-style pilsner, with the addition of corn. The corn gives it a sweeter flavor, more body. In Mexico, corn was cheaper than barley, and so it was frequently used." Light in color, it is fairly close to an American pale lager in taste. The other beer designed to move Las Cazuela's patrons to craft beer styles was Piedra del Fuego Stoned Cream Ale. The term "stoned" is not a reference to what happens to consumers of a non-liquid product sometimes called "Acapulco Gold." It signifies an important and infrequently used brewing process. After the mashing process, heated granite rocks are dropped into the newly created wort, caramelizing the sugars.

Chupacabra IPA is named after a legendary monster in Mexican folklore. At 7.2 percent ABV, it is one of Las Cazuela's strongest regular offerings. An American-style IPA, "it's not over-the-top bitter," Campbell noted. "We use Centennial, Chinook and Cascade hops. But I want people to taste the maltiness, so we have the barley to provide a strong background." For the hop aficionados who visit Las Cazuela's, he has created Papacabra (Father Cabra), a 9.3 percent ABV imperial IPA.

Other regular beers include a hefeweizen designed for those people who ask for Blue Moon, Coors's very popular wheat beer; a malty ESB inspired by Campbell's admiration of Red Hook Brewery's Northwest interpretation of the style; and Robusto Porter, which he says was designed to be like an Irish stout.

Limited editions include Beer for My Horse, an oatmeal stout that was named after a Willie Nelson song. Inebriator is a double bock. The 7.5 percent ABV beverage is, Campbell said laughingly, "like a candy bar in a glass that could knock you out. We made a small batch after we opened, and people keep asking when we're going to make it a regular."

SIERRA BLANCA BREWING COMPANY

1016 Industrial Loop, Moriarty, 87035
505-832-2337, www.sierrablancabrewery.com
Taproom: At the brewery and at ABQ Brewpub, 6601 Uptown Boulevard NE, Albuquerque.

Like many visitors to rural New Mexico, New Jersey natives Rich and Suzanne Weber liked the Land of Enchantment so much that they decided to move there. In the early 1990s, they settled happily in the mountain town of Ruidoso. There was, however, one thing that Rich Weber worried about. A beer lover, he couldn't find the wide selection of good beers he had enjoyed back east. He had discovered what he called "good beer" during a post-university trip to England. "A friend took me to some London pubs, and I tried all the beers. I particularly liked one called 'Old Peculiar,' an English dark ale. In fact, I liked it so much that I rented a car and drove to where it was brewed, a small city called Masham, not far from the Lake District."

Because of the difficulty in finding good beer in south-central New Mexico, Rich Weber decided that he'd start his own brewery. As a mechanical and electrical engineer, he'd be able to deal with the ordering and assembling of equipment. But making the beer would be a problem—he'd never brewed. So, he hired two experienced brewers, and for two years, he became their apprentice, learning as much as he could about the process of brewing.

He located the brewery—which he named Sierra Blanca, after a nearby 12,000-foot mountain—in Carrizozo, a small town a forty-minute drive from Ruidoso. "It wasn't too far from major transportation routes, building rentals were cheaper than in Ruidoso and the town was 1,200 feet lower in elevation than Ruidoso. So I would avoid a number of problems involved with high-altitude brewing."

The brewery opened in late 1996, offering an English brown ale, a pale ale and a lager. "There were a lot of Texas oil workers in the area, and they loved lagers." Then, in 1997, Sierra Blanca introduced the beer for which it has become famous: Roswell Alien Amber. The name celebrated the fiftieth anniversary of the supposed crash of an alien spaceship in southern New Mexico, and the label featured the head of a green extraterrestrial. A malty but not too sweet ale, and with a very low hop content, this smooth-tasting, medium-bodied ale offered newcomers to the craft brewing scene a flavorful, nonthreatening threshold beer, one that would move them away from mass-produced pale American lagers. It quickly became the brewery's best-selling product and still is, accounting for more than 50 percent of all sales.

Over the next decade, business grew steadily. By 2005, with an annual production at nearly 3,200 barrels, Sierra Blanca was the ninety-second-largest brewery in the United States. In addition to brewing its own beer, it did contract brewing for other breweries and also expanded distribution of its own beers from south-central New Mexico across the state and into neighboring states.

The space in Carrizozo soon became too small. Weber contacted other small brewers and talked to them about sharing space and equipment in a building in an industrial park in Moriarty, a town located thirty miles east of Albuquerque. The savings of sharing space and the convenience of being located only a few blocks from Interstate 40 convinced Abbey Brewing (then of Pecos, New Mexico) and Isotopes and Rio Grande Brewing (of Albuquerque) to join in the venture. However, just as the new facility was about to open in 2006, the owners of Rio Grande, Scott Moore and Tom Hart, offered to sell their brewery to Weber, who quickly accepted. The Rio Grande name would be kept, along with its Outlaw Lager and Pancho Verde Chili-Cerveza.

In 2010, Weber, in cooperation with restaurateur Adam Krafft, opened ABQ Brewpub in uptown Albuquerque. A gastro-brewpub, it serves at the brewery's taproom and also features a one-barrel system with which for several years Ben Miller, the winner of many national home-brewing awards, created small batches of unusual beers. Then, in 2012, Weber opened the Rio Grande Brew Pub and Grill, inside the Albuquerque SunPort Airport.

In addition to the beers produced for Isotopes Brewing, Abbey Beverage and De La Vega's Pecan Grill of Las Cruces, the Moriarty facilities brew

Rich Weber, head brewer and co-owner of Sierra Blanca Brewing Company, stands before the new logos for the brewery's Alien line of beers. *Courtesy the author.*

eleven Sierra Blanca products that range from a light pale American lager to an imperial stout. Sierra Blanca Light and New Mexico Lager, available only in draft, are, Weber noted, designed for the Bud drinkers; the lager also serves as the base beer for the chili-cerveza.

Four of the beers are sold under the Rio Grande label. Outlaw Lager is a California common (aka steam beer) brewed with lager yeast but fermented at ale temperatures. "That's why we call it 'Outlaw,'" Weber explained. "It doesn't obey the usual brewing laws." It has a caramelly, nutty flavor with very little hop presence. Desert Pilsner is a clear, crisp, clean-finishing brew that uses German and Czech (Saaz) hops. The two beers weigh in at 5.2 and 5.4 percent ABV, respectively. The IPA is the brewery's hoppiest beer at 78 International Bitterness Units (IBU). However, the bitterness is complemented by the citrusy notes, giving the beer an interesting complexity.

The most famous of the Rio Grande offerings is Pancho Verde Chili-Cerveza. The name, package design and advertising slogan pay tribute to well-known elements of New Mexico culture. "Pancho Verdi" is a not-so-subtle pun on Pancho Villa, a revolutionary Mexican general who invaded southern New Mexico early in the twentieth century. The stylized design on the label, the skull of a bull with green chiles for horns, depicted against a background of New Mexico desert and mountains, seems to be a humorous tribute to New Mexico's most famous artist, Georgia O'Keeffe. In addition to the lager base, it is created with 12 percent corn in the mash because, Weber remarked, "nothing goes with chile as well as corn." After the brewing is completed, large "tea bags" filled with whole roasted chiles are suspended into the brew. The result is a 4.7 percent ABV, well-rounded beer that has a lager crispness.

Three beers are marketed under the Alien label: Alien Amber, Alien Wheat and Alien Imperial Stout. The American-style wheat beer, introduced in 2010, uses red and white wheat, along with coriander and orange peel. Low in alcohol at 4.6 percent ABV and in bitterness at 12 IBUs, it quickly established itself as a summer favorite and is challenging Alien Amber as Sierra Blanca's best-selling beer. Alien Imperial Stout, the brewery's first entry into the big/strong beer category, is a creamy-bodied 8.3 percent ABV beverage with coffee and mocha notes. The slight hop finish prevents the malts from becoming too sweet. In 2012, the labels for the Alien brands were redesigned, with the green cartoon-like figure being replaced by a stark silvery mask with large, orange, oval eyes. "We wanted to pay tribute to the Dia de los Meurtos, an important Hispanic festival and part of New Mexico's cultural heritage," Weber noted.

The pale ale and nut brown ale use the Sierra Blanca label. Although it is categorized as an American style, the pale achieves a good hop-malt balance similar to English versions of the style. The nut brown ale is definitely in the English style and won the gold medal in its category at the 2012 Great American Beer Festival competition. German and English chocolate and caramel malts are used along with English Fuggles hops, giving a rich, rounded flavor.

Asked about the house style of Sierra Blanca's beers, Weber replied that there really wasn't one. "We use five different yeasts, and we want to offer a range of different beers. If we have any distinctive characteristic, I think that it's that most of our beers could be considered session beers—flavorful, well-rounded and not too high in alcohol."

Rich Weber is still as enthusiastic about brewing beer as he was more than a decade and a half ago. He plays a major, hands-on role in brewing, serving as head brewer when there is a temporary vacancy for the position. "My favorite time of the day," he declared, a note of excitement in his voice, "is in the early morning, just before sunrise. Nobody else is there. I put some music on, and for the next few hours, I have fun making beer."

TURTLE MOUNTAIN BREWING COMPANY

905 Thirty-sixth Street SE, Rio Rancho, 87124
505-994-9497, www.turtlemountainbrewing.com
Taproom: At the brewery.

When he was a high school student in Santa Fe, Nico Ortiz, the owner of Turtle Mountain Brewing in Rio Rancho, took part in a two-month study program in Germany. "I learned what really good beer was, and I experienced the wonderful German beer culture—the classic old breweries and the wonderful beer halls and beer gardens." That trip ignited Nico's lifelong passion for good beer. He visited breweries and brewpubs at home and abroad, enjoying a great variety of well-crafted lagers and ales and appreciating the environments, the tasting rooms, brewpubs and restaurants in which people gathered to drink beer together.

In 1991, after earning a master's degree in business from Northwestern University in Illinois, he returned to New Mexico and "realized I wanted to open a brewpub or at least a restaurant that brewed its own beer. A friend suggested Rio Rancho as a good location. It was a place that had the right demographics and not many restaurants. People who worked at Intel knew about craft beer and they had the income to buy beer that was a little more expensive than the megabrands. They also had families, so I had to have a restaurant for the whole family."

The name for Rio Rancho's oldest brewpub comes from the Tewa-language words *Oku Pin*, meaning "Turtle Mountain," the name of both the nearby Sandia Mountains and owner Nico Ortiz's father. *Courtesy Turtle Mountain Brewing Company.*

Nico decided to call his planned brewery Turtle Mountain. The name was taken from the Tewa-language words *Oku Pin*, meaning Turtle Mountain, the name of the Sandia Mountains and the Native name of his father, the respected anthropologist Alfonso Ortiz, who had provided both emotional and financial support for Nico's venture.

The opening of Turtle Mountain in 1999 came about because of what Nico Ortiz called "a weirdly fortuitous" series of events. "The people who owned a Rio Rancho laundromat decided to close; the space was just the right size for a restaurant and brew house. A fellow I was talking to at a beer-tasting event told me about some nearly new brewing equipment that was available in Tucson. Then I ran into an old friend who was in the food industry and asked if he could suggest someone to run the restaurant side of the business. He said he was interested." At just about the same time, Mark Matheson, a winemaker and brewer, resigned from his position as brewmaster at Assets Bar and Grill, an Albuquerque brewpub. Nico signed him up to be a member of the team.

In 1999, Nico Ortiz's dream became a reality. "It was pretty tough going at first," he remembered. "Not only did we have to make people aware of us, but we also had to get them to accept a new concept: a restaurant that brewed its own beers, beers that weren't like the pale yellow American lagers they were used to." Gradually, the restaurant developed a loyal clientele. "We needed more seating and more room to brew more beer," Ortiz remembered. "So we bought some vacant property a few blocks to the west and then built a bigger restaurant and brew house. We opened up in 2006 and have been here since."

The new restaurant features a small outdoor patio designed to avoid the wind that frequently blows through Rio Rancho. Inside, a bar, booths and tables are arranged so that patrons have a good view of the television sets, which are the center of attention during football games. Above the bar, a sign proclaims, "Who needs a born-on date when you're in the delivery room?"—a reference to the brewing date found on the bottles and cans of one of the major American brewers. Bar towels from around England and Europe adorn one wall, while circular serving trays advertising American and international breweries cover another.

The menu offers fairly standard family restaurant fare: chicken wraps, soup and salad, several varieties of pizza, calzones, grinders, burgers, chicken, mac 'n' cheese and fish 'n' chips, as well as an eight-ounce sirloin. Among the appetizers are several items with a New Mexico slant, including tortilla chips and wings with habanero stout barbecue sauce. Among the extra toppings for the pizzas are green chiles, poblano peppers, fresh jalapeños and roasted red peppers.

There is no fixed list of year-round beers. "We like to offer a wide variety of styles and variations of style," Ortiz explained. "We make sure that we have one lighter beer, something in the amber range, something hoppy and something dark. When something Mark brews is really popular, we offer it more frequently." There have been nearly a dozen IPAs, including 5-C IPA (a reference to the number of hops beginning with the letter *C* used in the brew), Oaked Hoptimus IPA (a barrel-aged IPA) and Wild Bill Hiccup's Oatmeal IPA. Although twelve of the fifty-seven beers on Rate Beer website's list of consumer ratings are 5.0 percent ABV or under, there are plenty of big beers: nine in the 7.0 percent ABV range, four in the 8.0 percent range and five that are over 9.0 percent, including Evil Sister and Oblivion Express, barley wines that weigh in at 14.5 percent and 11.6 percent ABV, respectively.

Mark Matheson, the man in charge of making the beers, was a high school home-brewer who was turned on to the great possibilities of brewing when he acquired a first-edition copy of Charlie Papazian's *The Complete Joy of Home Brewing*, a classic in the field. He studied fermentation science at the University of California–Davis, not far from his home of Stockton. But after graduation, he spent as much time making wine as brewing beer. "Most Davis students were headed for careers in the big breweries. I didn't want to work for Budweiser because I liked small operations where I could become involved in all aspects." He divided his time working at small breweries and wineries in California and New Mexico. He recalled that when Ortiz called, "I wasn't sure I wanted to get back to brewing because I was getting more involved with making wine. But my wife suggested I give it a try." He did, and fourteen years later, was still on the job.

Matheson commented on the beers that could be called Turtle Mountain regulars. About IPAs in general, he noted that they "drive the craft industry here; they drive the train. They are particularly good with the spicy foods that are so popular in New Mexico." About Cabo Lager, he noted that while a brewpub must have a lager, something that can serve as what is often called a "training beer" for novices, making Cabo is extremely difficult. "Lagers are generally more difficult to make than ales, but in Rio Rancho, the water has been getting progressively harder and you need soft water for lager. We're reducing the pH of the water and looking for a good soft-water yeast. Cabo is like a Dortmunder Export, a little fuller in body and maltier than a pilsner." It is served with a slice of lime to remind patrons of the Mexican beers they know.

Red Rye, one of the first and still one of the most popular Turtle Mountain beers, is a variation on a red ale recipe that Matheson developed while working at Assets. "We use about 15 percent malted rye in the mash, which gives chocolaty and spicy notes to the beer. When we opened, New Belgium's Fat Tire had come to New Mexico and was hugely popular. We wanted to provide the Red Rye as an alternative."

While Matheson remarked that at Turtle Mountain, "we're all hops and malts," he's not above having fun by adding different flavorings to his beers. Perhaps the most interesting is Summer Scotch, at 4.5 percent ABV, a surprisingly mild version of the style. The additives perk it up: mugwort, heather tips and rosehips.

CHAPTER 5

SANTA FE

BLUE CORN CAFÉ & BREWERY

4056 Cerrillos Road, Santa Fe, 87507
505-438-1800, www.bluecorncafe.com
Taprooms: At the brewery and Blue Corn Café (downtown), 133 West Water Street,
Santa Fe.

During a three-year period in the mid-1990s, the number of brewpubs in the United States increased by 72 percent. One of the new brewpubs was founded by the owners of the Santa Fe Dining group, who decided to open a second location for their Blue Corn Café and to install in it a brew house that would provide beer for both locations.

The original Blue Corn Café was located a five-minute walk from Santa Fe's historic plaza. The new restaurant/brewery, which opened in 1997, would be in Century Plaza, at the corner of the very busy south Santa Fe intersection of Cerrillos and Rodeo Roads. The location would attract shoppers in the complex, would serve people in the rapidly expanding southern parts of Santa Fe and would be easily accessible to tourists driving into and out of the "City Different." In addition to New Mexican–style cooking and standard pub grub, it would offer patrons a chance to enjoy

In addition to its award-winning beers, Blue Corn offers its patrons what it calls "New Mexico specialties and contemporary comfort food." *Courtesy the author.*

beers that were brewed behind the full-length glass windows at the back of the dining room.

Laure Pomianowski, one of a relatively small number of female brewers in the craft brewing industry, was chosen to develop recipes and brew Blue Corn's beers. An engineer by training, she had worked at Santa Fe Brewing Company during its early years and then became the owner of a home-brewers' supply store. Her first beer offerings for Blue Corn revealed the nature of the New Mexico craft beer culture of the time: Atomic Blonde Ale, Bee Sting Honey Wheat (the name had to be changed when the company received a "cease and desist" order), End of the Trail Brown and Plaza Porter. It was a relatively safe list, unthreatening to those who considered Corona a high-end beer. The blonde ale (later transformed into a lager), 40K Honey Wheat Ale (the new name) and End of the Trail Brown are still around, although the recipes have been tweaked by a succession of brewers. Noticeably absent from the initial list was an India pale ale. The New Mexico passion for big-hopped beers was a six-pack or more of years away.

Since the departure of Laure Pomianowski, the names of the brewers who learned, honed or perfected their craft at the still-operational seven-barrel brew house behind the glass windows reads like a who's who of the New Mexico craft brewing industry: Ted Rice, Daniel Jaramillo, Justin Hamilton, John Bullard, Jordy Dralle and Brad Kraus. The brew house almost closed in 2008. It was expected that the newly opened Marble Brewery in Albuquerque would supply beer for the two Blue Corn restaurants and that the space occupied by the brewing equipment at Cerillos and Rodeo would be converted into a private dining room. However, demand for Marble beer grew so rapidly that the Albuquerque brewery could not supply product for its northern neighbors, and after four months, the Blue Corn facility was pressed back into operation.

Blue Corn Brewery does not look very different from when it opened in 1997. To the left of the entrance is the sports bar, with five televisions. Laminated onto the tabletops of the booths are logos of Blue Corn beers past and present. Three large copper vessels, which serve as bright/conditioning tanks next to the bar, provide visible evidence that brewing is going on somewhere in the building. A two-sided fireplace separates the sports bar and the dining room, which looks out onto a small patio. In front of the large glass windows separating the dining room and brew house are four large wooden barrels in which current brewer John Bullard is aging special limited editions of a Russian imperial stout and a wheat-based Belgian-style sour beer.

The menu defines the food as "gourmet New Mexican." There are plenty of dishes that come with chipotle, jalapeño or green chile sauces, as well as those standard New Mexico dishes green chile stew and green chile cheeseburgers. A special section of the menu specifically termed "New Mexican" includes enchiladas, burritos, tacos, tomales, rellenos, carne adovada and chimichangas.

Brewer John Bullard is officially a graduate of the American Brewers Guild and unofficially of the Blue Corn/Marble/Chama River training program. A New Mexico native—he was born in the town of Edgewood— he was a loyal Bud and Pabst Blue Ribbon drinker until the day a friend took him to Chama River's downtown Albuquerque taproom. "I tried their amber beer and was amazed by the flavor. After that, I spent a lot of time there." He also began to home-brew (very hoppy ales) in his studio apartment and, he confesses, "started to harass Ted Rice every week for a job at Marble." His persistence paid off; he became a deliveryman for the brewery, a job that paid considerably less than he had been earning at a local supermarket. But he was happy.

After two months, he received a promotion to keg cleaner and later became a brewing assistant at Chama River in Albuquerque and then at Blue Corn. At these places, he was mentored by Jeff Erway and Daniel Jaramillo, respectively. Then came the official training at the American Brewers Guild, followed by more hands-on brewing experience at Marble, where his teacher was Ted Rice, and Chama River.

Blue Corn offers six year-round beers, along with rotating seasonals. Three are designed for the entry-level craft beer drinker. Atomic Blonde Lager, a 5.0 percent ABV German pilsner, uses Saaz hops, more frequently found in Bohemian pilsners, to give "a slightly hopped-up finish." 40K Honey Wheat Ale, a descendant of the original Bee Sting, is an American wheat beer and uses local honey. The 5.6 percent ABV beverage is, Bullard noted, "somewhat like Marble's Wildflower Wheat, except that we add coriander and orange peel." Atalaya Amber (named after a Santa Fe area mountain) uses caramel, pale and toasted malts with a variety of hops to provide a balanced 5.5 percent ABV, 30 IBU ale.

Road Runner IPA, a beer that probably wouldn't have been considered for inclusion on Blue Corn's list a decade and a half ago, is a 6.8 percent ABV, 90 IBU rendering of this West Coast style. "We use eight hop varieties to give it bitterness, flavor and aroma," Bullard explained before adding, with a smile on his face, "but it's quite restrained compared to Jeff's." He's referring to mentor Erway's very strong, very hoppy, multi-award-winning Elevated IPA. Road Runner is Blue Corn's best-selling beer.

In 2013, Bullard's other two regular brews brought him national attention. Both End of the Trail Brown Ale and Gold Medal Stout (named after the beer that won a first-place medal in 2007) won silver medals in the American-Style Brown Ale and Oatmeal Stout categories, respectively, at the Great American Beer Festival. End of the Trail (5.6 percent ABV, 25 IBUs) is, John explained, hoppier and more robust than the English version of the style. He then confessed that he worked on the recipe after he had entered the name of the beer in the competition. "I changed it to something I thought was better. In fact, it's the only Blue Corn recipe that I've ever made significant changes to." Gold Medal Stout is somewhat English in style. Smooth-bodied, with coffee and caramel notes, it includes some hops to slightly cut the sweetness.

"The house lineup of beers pays the bill," Bullard noted. "The others are fun—challenges and a chance to play around, to experiment." He pointed to the wine and bourbon barrels in front of the brewing area, talked about their contents and then discussed Blue Corn Resurgence, the winner of the New Mexico 2013 IPA Challenge. The recipe included Citra, Simcoe and

Centennial hops, all well-known varieties, along with Eldorado hops, a new variety noted for the tropical fruit flavors it produces. Resurgence was the first non-Albuquerque entry to win the annual statewide summer competition.

When Blue Corn first started brewing its own beer, John Bullard was only thirteen years old, perhaps "borrowing" a Bud or Blue Ribbon from the family fridge. Sixteen years later, in 2013, he was maintaining the high standards of his predecessors and mentors and, as the awards won in that year indicate, making significant contributions to the traditions they established.

DUEL BREWING

1228 Parkway Drive, Santa Fe, 87507
505-474-5301, www.duelbrewing.com
Taproom: At the brewery.

When Trent Edwards decided to create a brewpub/production brewery specializing in Belgian-style beers, he felt that it "would bring together all my skills and experiences." He'd been a businessman, a painter, a sculptor and a home-brewer. "This was the most difficult thing I ever did," he said, after the project was completed in 2013 and Duel Brewing was operational.

The steps involved in creating a brewery reflected the idea of the creative process expressed by one of Edwards's favorite artists and thinkers, French-American painter and sculptor Marcel Duchamp: "In the creative act, the artist goes from intention to realization through a chain of totally subjective reactions. His struggle toward the realization is a series of efforts, pains, satisfaction, refusals [and] decisions." In fact, Edwards views the creation of both Belgian beers and the brewpub in which people experience them as a kind of art. "Drinking Belgian beers is not a minimal experience," he explained. The creative experience, like the experience of viewing a painting, is not complete until the drinker has responded sensitively to the nuances of the Belgian beer style he or she is sipping.

The environment in which the sipping takes place is part of this completion of the creative experience. The Duel brewpub is located in an industrial area several blocks from one of the city's main thoroughfares, Cerillos Avenue. A small sign above the entrance identifies the establishment. Inside, some of Edwards's own paintings adorn the walls. The counter on which the serving taps are mounted is a large, late nineteenth-century hutch, with original glass in the cabinet doors. There are no television sets; this is a place for either contemplation or quiet conversation. General Manager Matt Onstott laughingly recalled an incident that occurred during the 2013 World Series. "A man came in, ordered a beer and then started looking around. Then he asked me where the television sets were. When I told him we had none, he got up and left without even touching his beer." Food is also a part of the experience, and in the small kitchen tucked into a corner of the three-barrel brew house, Belgian waffles, the house specialty, are made.

Brewer Todd Yocham is a trained graphic artist and a former home-brewer. Describing himself as a brewer, he jokingly said, "I have a complex," and then went on to say that he designs beers that are complex. "We don't make a beer that isn't complex." At Duel, the beers are served in tulip-shaped glasses and snifters "because we want people to sip, to slow down and enjoy the complex flavors."

Although most of the beers are very strong, three of them are 6 percent ABV or less. Bad Amber is named after a painting by sixteenth-century German painter Lucas Cranach the Elder. "By bad, we mean wickedly delicious," reads the menu description of this 5.9 percent ABV Belgian amber. Light- to medium-bodied, it is crisp and clean. "The yeasts and malts complement each other," Yocham noted. Duchamp (named after Marcel) Sour Wit is a 5.2 percent ABV beverage. "The yeast really plays with the bitter orange we add during the boil," said Yocham. Non-Fiction is a 5.2 percent ABV Belgian pale ale. The use of English hops helps to create a balance between the flavors of the malts, yeast and hops.

The big beers include Fiction, a 7.1 percent ABV Belgian IPA. The name is a reference to French novelist Albert Camus' statement about fiction being the means of telling the truth. Titian, a Belgian strong ale (8.1 percent ABV), is named after the painter famous for depicting redheaded women. Yocham said that although the recipe is simple, the brewing process is complex. "We use a variety of malts and go through a four-step mashing process." Dark Ryder, an 11.0 percent ABV strong dark ale, is named after the late nineteenth-century artist Albert Pinkham Ryder, who was noted for his darkly allegorical paintings. Medium-bodied, it has chocolate notes from the malts and plum flavors from the yeast.

In the summer of 2013, shortly after the long process of creating a brewpub was completed and Duel was open for business, Trent Edwards was standing behind the bar looking happily at a room full of people who were obviously enjoying their evening's experience. "My wife phoned and wanted to know when I was coming home. I told her not for a while. I wanted to enjoy the experience, the happiness of having finished my part of the creative process and seeing other people complete it."

SANTA FE BREWING COMPANY

35 Fire Place, Santa Fe, 87508
505-424-3333, www.santafebrewing.com
Taprooms: At the brewery and at Eldorado Tap House, 7 Caliente Road, Unit 9A, Eldorado.

Founded in 1988, Santa Fe Brewing Company, New Mexico's first and longest-running craft brewery, did not begin operations in the "City Different." Its first home was on the outskirts of the nearby village of Galisteo in a horse barn at Flying M Ranch, owned by Mike Levis, a breeder of racehorses and seller of wine bottles to the growing number of New Mexico wineries.

As Ty Levis, Mike's son, remembered it, his father began to wonder why there were so many small wineries popping up in New Mexico and no microbreweries. Then he saw an ad for a used brewing system offered by Boulder Beer, Colorado's first microbrewery, and decided to buy it. With the help of Boulder Brewing's Mike Lawrence, he set the equipment up in the cramped quarters of the barn and began brewing. "When bottling time came," said Ty, who got his first job at the brewery as a bottle washer and is now director of brewing operations, "we had a machine that could cap only one bottle at a time, and we had to label each bottle individually."

While Ty washed empties and capped full bottles, Mike was visiting liquor stores and bars around Santa Fe and Albuquerque, selling Santa Fe Brewing's first three products: a bottle-conditioned pale ale, an American wheat ale and a nut brown ale. During the first year of production, just over five hundred barrels were brewed, and Mike established more than one hundred accounts.

In 1990, a fourth style was added to the Santa Fe list: a barley wine, the naming of which has given legendary status to one of the Flying M's barnyard animals. While members of the brewery staff were standing around trying to find a suitable name for the new brew, Petey (in some versions called Charlie), a dachshund (in some versions a miniature dachshund), ran amok, killing twenty barnyard chickens (some versions say twenty-seven and that the chickens belonged to a neighbor). His actions inspired the struggling namers, and Chicken Killer Barley Wine was born. The bottle labels still depict a gun-slinging dog standing menacingly, his paws resting on two six-shooters.

Over the next few years, production at Santa Fe remained relatively constant, around 750 barrels annually. By the mid-1990s, Mike Levis was expressing interest in selling Santa Fe. Brian Lock—a twenty-six-year-old native of Portland, Oregon, who had early fallen in love with craft beer, become a home-brewer and decided that his goal in life was to own his own brewery or brewpub—was interested. He had earned a business degree at Southern Methodist University located in the (then) beer wasteland of Dallas and, after graduation, returned to Oregon. He was working at a local microbrewery when college friends from New Mexico suggested that he move to a place where the weather was sunnier, drier and warmer. Lock and the two buddies, Carlos Muller and Dave Forester, talked about opening a brewpub in Santa Fe. But when they heard that the Blue Corn Restaurant and Brewery was scheduled to open, they decided that the city's beer culture wasn't big enough yet to support two brewpubs. Instead, the three friends, along with Ty Levis, bought a production brewery: Santa Fe.

The partners soon discovered that if they wanted to expand production beyond the 750 or so barrels per year, they would have to increase brewing capacity beyond what was possible at the ranch. In 1997, they moved the brewery to Dinosaur Trail, just adjacent to Interstate 25, south of Santa Fe, and set up an enlarged brew house in what had been a shop for the restoration of antique motorcycles. By 2004, they had increased annual production to 1,750 barrels, 87 percent of total capacity, and product was being distributed throughout New Mexico and in a few Colorado locations.

At this time, Lock began to develop plans to transform Santa Fe Brewing into a regional brewing company. First, he bought out his three partners, consolidating the decision-making process. Then he and his father bought the grounds on which had stood the recently bankrupted Wolf Canyon Brewing and leased it to his brewing company. "It was very close to a freeway. The land came with water rights, which meant we could use natural well water that didn't have the chemicals found in city water. And there was plenty of room for us to build a plant that had the size to hold the amount of equipment we'd need to brew enough beer to expand our out-of-state markets."

Production increased rapidly. By 2008, Santa Fe was producing 5,000 barrels. Output grew by 25 percent, 19 percent and 44 percent over the

Owner Brian Lock and Director of Brewing Operations Ty Levis stand beside one of the brewery's original tanks and in front of a recently purchased fermenter. *Courtesy the author.*

next three years, respectively. In 2011, the brewery put out 13,510 barrels and reached 20,000 in 2013. Santa Fe had become a regional brewery, selling in New Mexico, Colorado, Arizona, Texas, Missouri, Kansas, Oklahoma and Nevada.

Lock attributed this dramatic growth to the decision to package beer in cans as well as bottles. Although cans had long been used by the megabrewers, the cost of a canning line and the purchase of a very large quantity of cans had put canning beyond the reach of microbrewers. In addition, some brewers and a great number of beer snobs thought that canning beer was something only the big brewers did and thus unworthy of the craft brewing industry. But canning had now become less expensive, and more and more microbreweries were packaging in cans. The beer kept fresher longer, the plastic lining in cans prevented a metallic taste from creeping into the beer, cans were more environmentally friendly than glass bottles and they were easier and less expensive to transport.

In 2010, the year Santa Fe released Happy Camper, a new version of its IPA, in cans, production rose by more than 1,000 barrels and the next year by 3,300. Nearly half of the beer Santa Fe now brews is sold in cans. "We're brewing constantly," Ty Levis said. "But our canned beer is so popular we can barely keep up with demand."

Currently, Santa Fe has seven beers available all year, two of which have been around since 1988. The recipe for the American-style pale ale is basically the original one, with slight tinkering. Ty Levis described it as a "balanced beer, much like an American-style extra special bitter." The hops do not overwhelm and are complemented by the malts. Nut Brown Ale is medium-bodied, with understated coffee notes. Malty sweetness is modified by the hops, which give a slight tang. The original American-style wheat beer, designed as a crossover or "training-wheels" beer, has been replaced by a hefeweizen, which, in addition to the yeast notes, has more body than its predecessor.

State Pen Porter (named after a building not too far from the brewery) is, Brian Lock noted, an international-style porter, not as robust as the English style. There are coffee notes and some hop bitterness to counteract the malts. At 6.4 percent ABV, it is stronger than the pale, wheat and brown but not so strong as Java Imperial Stout, a full-bodied 8 percent ABV ale that uses blends of two organic coffees, one from East Timor and the other from Papua New Guinea. The strongest of the regulars is the ale the dog made famous, Chicken Killer Barley Wine, dark, full-bodied, flavorful and as powerful as a dachshund running amok in a barnyard. It is 10 percent ABV.

The newest of the regulars, Happy Camper IPA, Santa Fe's first canned beer and the one that has driven the skyrocketing sales since 2010, is a variation of the brewery's original IPA. Levis noted that it is strong (6.6 percent ABV) and hoppy "but not over the top." It is refreshing but not too dry, and it has malt undertones that keep the hoppiness under control. "We spent a lot of time on the recipe," Lock explained. "We needed something that would hold up well in cans, which, when people packed them in coolers, would not be as cold as they would in a refrigerator. Even though they might be a little warmer, the beer still keeps its complex flavors."

The seasonal offerings include Black IPA (winter), a hearty 7.1 percent ABV beer in which the citrusy hop flavors dominate but don't overwhelm the presence of the dark malts; Irish Red (spring); Freestyle Pilsner (summer), a Bohemian-style pilsner that, at 5.5 percent ABV, is stronger than its European counterparts; and Oktoberfest.

Santa Fe has also joined the ranks of brewers that produce Belgian-style sours and lambics that are conditioned in barrels. These beers are issued in a limited-edition series named "Los Innovadores" and are packaged in 750mL swing top bottles, each of which is hand-labeled, numbered and signed. The 2013 batch was a Kriek, a sour ale with cherries added.

By brewing 20,000 barrels in 2013, Santa Fe Brewing increased its production by more than 320 percent in five years. Brian Lock looks to even greater growth in the years to come. "We have good beer, and the name Santa Fe, along with our Zia sun logo [which also appears on the state flag], is a wonderful marketing device. We have ordered more brewing equipment, and we hope to expand into more states." And he wonders aloud whether an annual production figure of 200,000 barrels might be reachable in the not-too-distant future.

SECOND STREET BREWERY

1814 Second Street, Santa Fe, 87501
505-982-3030, www.secondstreetbrewery.com
Taproom: At the brewery and at Second Street Brewery at the Railyard, 1607 Paseo de Peralta #10, Santa Fe.

In the mid-1990s, Peter Allen, a Santa Fe architect and, more important for beer lovers, a member of the "Grainful Heads," a home-brew club, decided

This coaster lists just a few of the wide variety of beers offered by Second Street. *Courtesy Second Street Brewery.*

that the "City Different" needed a brewpub. There were brewpubs in Taos, Albuquerque, Las Cruces and even Elephant Butte, but the area's only brewery, Santa Fe Brewing, was a production facility located out of town in Galisteo. Allen launched a successful drive to sign up thirty investors at $15,000 each and found a suitable place for his brewery, a former fireplace, wood stove and hot tub outlet, located on Second Street.

At the same time, he found his brewer, Rob Tweet, a recent graduate from the American Brewers Guild in Davis, California. Tweet had been an industrial engineer in Oregon who had been home-brewing for several years before deciding to make a career change. He'd been introduced to craft brews in college. "I was camping with friends at Lake Shasta in California. One of the guys bought a six-pack of Sierra Nevada Pale Ale and put it in the cooler. That night, I drank it all." After his formal studies, Tweet apprenticed at Humboldt Brewing in northern California. He became Second Street's head brewer in 1996 and was named president in 2000.

When he arrived in Santa Fe, New Mexico's craft beer culture was, Tweet remembered, "pretty primitive." Between 1988, when Santa Fe Brewing started up, and the end of 1995, only twelve breweries and brewpubs had opened. One had already closed, and another six of them would cease operations by 2000. When Second Street opened in 1996, beer drinkers' palates had not yet developed the love of hops that would begin to dominate the New Mexico scene in the opening years of the twenty-first century. "I remember the first beer I made. It was an English pale ale, and it was too much for people. I had to lighten it up." Nonetheless, Second Street's beers began to catch on. "We had to brew constantly to keep up with the demand. And we had good food too."

Second Street is a neighborhood type of brewpub, a quiet, out-of-the-way gathering place where friends can get together and can bring their families. The place became so popular that in 1998, the decision was made to add a patio to increase seating during the warm months. The patio remains a feature of the brewpub, the large trees providing a shady canopy that gives the area the feeling of a secluded courtyard. The increased popularity of Second Street soon rendered the original restaurant and brewery inadequate. So, in 2004, a building just north of the brewpub was purchased and renovated to house a seven-barrel brewing system. The space that had been occupied by the brewing equipment, very cramped quarters behind the restaurant, was remodeled to increase the seating. Between 2008 and 2012, annual beer production increased by 40 percent, from 1,200 barrels to more than 1,700.

At the time that the new brew house, with its increased capacity, was being built, Tweet, now one of the owners, along with other members of the ownership group, began considering a second Second Street. Tweet was particularly attracted to the Railyard District, the site of Santa Fe's original railroad station. By the 1980s, it had been declared a blighted area, and community leaders and civic officials began to consider ways it could be revitalized. In 2002, a master plan was developed, and in 2008, it opened with a farmers' market, restaurants, galleries, cultural centers and trendy shops. "I had Second Street on the list for a lease should a suitable place come up. We connected with the farmers' market group and rented space in their building," Tweet said. "Many of the people who shop there come to

President and Head Brewer Rob Tweet stands underneath plaques listing many of the beers that he has created for Second Street Brewery. *Courtesy the author.*

our place for a meal and a beer. We try to buy as much of our food from the farmers' market. We opened in 2010, and some people wondered whether the economic recession would hurt us, but we've done very well."

The menu at both locations has been described as "New Mexico–style pub grub." There are salsas and corn chips, red or green chile cheese fries, green chile chicken stew, a chile philly, a jalapeño cheddar sausage wrap and enchiladas. Fish and chips, that staple of English pub menus, is also available. Desserts include the classic "comfort" dessert bread pudding, as well as a stout brownie. The Farmer's Plate Special, available only at the Railyard, includes locally made sausage, chutney and cheese that has been purchased next door.

Hanging from beams at the original Second Street are wooden plaques listing the names of the beers that Rob Tweet and his assistants have brewed since 1996. There are well over fifty of these plaques, listing beers from alt to weizenbock. "I like formulating recipes, coming up with new things. I enjoy the process that goes from visualization to realization," said Tweet. After brewing the English pale that some customers found too much, he created a robust IPA, an ESB and a cream stout. The cream stout attracted attention not just from the locals but also from the judges at the 1997 Great American Beer Festival, where it won a bronze medal in the Oatmeal Stout category.

Looking at the plaques, it's surprising to see how many versions of English bitter, pale ale and IPA there are: ten pale ales and five each of bitter and IPA. "I really like to play around with hops," Tweet confessed. "I think that America pale ale is the best style to show up the qualities of hops. Whenever a new hop comes on the market, I experiment with it to see what's 'hoppening.' Many of the pales on the list are single-hopped beers, brewed to showcase the characteristics of one hop. Some of them I only try once, others I brew again." One of his hoppy beers came into being by accident and, in 2013, won a bronze medal at the Great American Beer Festival in the American-Style Amber Lager category. Tweet had ordered some of the British ale yeast he used in Rod's Best Bitter, but by mistake, the supplier sent him a lager yeast. "I certainly wasn't going to waste it, so I turned the temperature down to sixty degrees Fahrenheit, used fewer bittering hops and the result was something like a California common, like the steam beer Anchor makes. It became a very big seller."

One of the big changes that Tweet has noticed in the microbrewing scene over the last two decades relates to lagers. "At first, you didn't see many of them," he said. "They took so long to make, and they took up too much tank space. Breweries just starting up couldn't afford to have a beer sit for six or more weeks until it was ready to serve. Now everyone expects you to have a lager." And his list has included Tres Equis Lager (a Mexican-style beer), a schwarzbier (a German beer made with dark malts), a maibock, an Oktoberfest and a Bohemian pilsner.

Lest patrons become overwhelmed by the rotating beer list, Second Street has three core beers that people can expect to see every time they visit. The simply titled IPA is 6 percent ABV and 60 IBUs, relatively modest by contemporary standards. Not surprisingly, it illustrates Tweet's love of hops. Magnum, Columbus, Centennial, Cascade and Crystal varieties contribute a subtle range of flavors and aromas. "I also use crystal malts to give a firm malty background. I consider it a West Coast–style IPA, with a touch of English thrown in."

Kolsch is almost the direct opposite of the IPA: light in body and color, low in alcohol and hop bitterness. The 4.6 percent ABV beer has a slightly sweet though not cloying taste, with a clean, crisp finish and a few nutty malt notes. The refreshing hop notes are contributed by the Vanguard hops, an American variety that bears some similarity to the Hallertau hops of Germany.

The recipe for the award-winning stout is, Tweet noted, very complicated. Seven different malts and a British yeast give it a roasty character, with chocolate and caramel notes. "It's a full, complex drink," he said. The use of English Fuggles hops provides an earthy, not-too-bitter contrast to the rich malt flavors. "It's a great dessert beer," he remarked enthusiastically.

Describing the characteristics that underlie the tremendous variety of styles that have been brewed at Second Street, Tweet said, "I really like the hop character of our beers, but I like the beers to be balanced and not extreme. I like them to have a dry finish. We've done many different kinds of beer, but I'd say we lean toward English styles."

CHAPTER 6
TAOS

ESKE'S BREW PUB & EATERY

106 Des Georges Place, Taos, 87571
575-758-1517, www.eskesbrewpub.com
Taproom: At the brewery.

When Steve Eskeback moved to Taos in 1982, he brought with him a love of good skiing and good beer. He'd been a member of the ski patrol in Washington State, and trip to England had introduced him to British pub life and to ales that were a lot better than Rainier Ale, a beer that the people of the Pacific Northwest referred to, not affectionately, as "The Green Death."

He found wonderful skiing in northern New Mexico and became a member of the ski patrol at Taos Ski Valley. However, he didn't find the beer scene very impressive. "You had to drive to Albuquerque if you wanted to buy Sierra Nevada," remembered Eske, as everyone calls him. And so he chose the best alternative to the long drive: he became a home-brewer. "I had the use of the kitchen at the Phoenix, the food service company at the ski hill, so I started brewing there." He was very good at and very enthusiastic about his hobby, so much so Wanda Anderson, his wife, asked what he was going to do with what had become a nearly all-consuming passion.

"We decided to look at the brewpub scene in Oregon, Washington and British Columbia. After the visit, we agreed that our beers were as good as and sometimes better than most of the ones we'd tried." That's when he decided to turn the passion into a profession. One day, late in the 1980s, while he was visiting Embudo Station Restaurant, twenty miles south of Taos, the owner, Preston Cox, asked if he could buy some of Eske's beer. Eske agreed, and after he took one hundred bottles to the restaurant, it was so popular that it sold in two days.

Eske formed Sangre de Cristo Brewing, set up his brewing equipment in a small building fifty yards from the Embudo Station Restaurant and began to create beers for the restaurant. One of the first brews has, over the past two decades, become a classic and the flagship for Sangre de Cristo: a green chile beer. In a state where the official state question is "Red or Green," referring to which chile patrons wish with their meals, he knew that he had to make a good beer. He did, and it was named "Best in Show" at the 1990 New Mexico State Fair Pro-Am beer competition.

He enjoyed brewing at Embudo Station but wanted to base his operations in Taos, his home. In 1992, Steve and Wanda moved their equipment back to Taos and opened the town's first brewpub: Eske's Brew Pub & Eatery. "I really wanted it to be in the British style, where people could enjoy good food and beer, where families could gather. I wanted it to be a community meeting place." They chose what had been an eighty-year-old house near the center of town. The onetime residence of the prominent Des Georges family, it had character and was just the right size for the kind of brewpub the couple had envisioned. "We had trouble with the name Sangre de Cristo Brewing. Some officials thought it was sacrilegious, But cooler heads prevailed. Because of the place's historical status, we weren't permitted to make many changes, although we were allowed to do some excavation in the basement to make room for our brewing equipment."

"The first year was rough going," Eske remembered. "We were offering something new to the area, and we had to be educators. Fortunately, many of our early customers were tourists who had come to ski and who knew about craft beer." One of the tourists was Michael Jackson, the world-famous beer writer. He'd visited Embudo Station and written about the chile beer, ESB and stout that Eske had brewed. And then, shortly after Eske's opened, Jackson returned to Taos. "We had two or three other brewers present," Eske remembered. "Jackson tried our beers and made lots of notes."

The brewpub looks pretty much as it did in 1992. The biggest change is a large shaded patio just off the south-facing porch. Inside, the small kitchen is still presided over by Wanda Anderson. In addition to such southwestern favorites as "The Fatty," a wheat tortilla that includes green chile turkey stew, and the green chile burrito, there is a gluten-free green chile stew and a gluten-free Mediterranean salad sampler. Weekly specials include a "Blue Plate Special" (southern comfort food), fish and chips, sushi and "World Eats."

More than thirty different styles of beer are brewed during a year. Although there are some West Coast–style beers, Eske's is not, as former brewer Chris Jones remarked, "into shock and awe with our beers." Since the summer of 2013, the responsibility for brewing the various offerings has belonged to Cord Kiessling, a onetime underaged home-brewer from Westchester, New York. He'd come to Taos in 2008 and had been working as a bartender at the brewpub when Jones tendered his resignation. Kiessling had been considering a move to Denver to take a brewing position there when he heard the news. He decided to stay at Eske's.

One of the beers that is always on tap is the Taos Green Chile Beer, which won a Great American Beer Festival bronze medal in 1993 and is still brewed according to the recipe Eske developed more than two decades ago. It is built on the base of a blonde ale that does not intrude on the chile taste. The finished beer has a moderately intense chile flavor with some heat. So famous has Eske's Taos Green Chile Beer become that it is used as the example of the style in an article about beer adjuncts on Wikipedia.

In addition to Taos Green Chile beer, a dozen other styles are regularly on tap. Blonde Betty, designed for entry-level craft beer drinkers, and Hoola Hoop Hefe, an American-style wheat, are the lightest beers. Artist Ale, a Northwest take on an English bitter, is based on a long-ago Washington State favorite of Eske's, Ballard Bitter. Special Bitter is more in the style of an English ESB. The three pale ale offerings range from Mesa Pale Ale, which has more body than is typical of the style; Millennium IPA, a strong beer at 6.2 percent ABV; and Mr. Personality, an imperial IPA that former brewer Chris Jones described as being in the line of Stone Brewing's Arrogant Bastard IPA.

The dark beers include Eske's Brown Ale, a sweetish English-style ale that, at 4.0 percent ABV, is a popular session beer; Oat Cole Porter, a creamy and sweet Irish-style stout; a 6.0 percent Scottish ale, a wee heavy beer with a hearty balance of malts and hops; and 10,000 Foot Stout, which Eske said was influenced by the late Bert Grant, a legendary Washington State brewer. The name comes from the elevation of the Phoenix kitchen in which Eske first experimented with the stout recipe and others.

Now having been open for more than two decades, Eske's is the longest-operating New Mexico brewpub. A favorite with the locals, many of whom bring their families to enjoy the various dinner specials, it is also sought out by tourists. A check of the ratings on Rate Beer and Beer Advocate, two consumer response websites, reveals that comments come not only from in the country but also from Canada, Europe and other places around the globe.

TAOS ALE HOUSE

401 Paseo Del Pueblo Norte, Taos. 87571
575-758-5522, www.taosalehouse.com
Taproom: At the brewery.

Jesse Cook, the owner, brewmaster and, as he puts it, "chief toilet scrubber" of Taos Ale House, is, like the operators of many small New Mexico breweries, the beneficiary of a state law that allows in-state breweries to sell their products directly to one another. "I like variety, but I don't have the brewing capacity to supply twelve taps. Buying other New Mexico beers allows me to have that variety, and I can help people discover just how many wonderful beers are being brewed in the state."

Jesse had studied biochemistry in college and had worked in many labs, experiences he said helped him when he began brewing. "That and the fact that I'd done a lot of cooking." He'd been a Bud drinker as a student, and it wasn't until he'd moved to Southern California to become a furniture builder that he discovered the wonderful array of craft beers that were available.

When business slowed in California, Cook moved to his wife's hometown of Taos and began to frequent Eske's, New Mexico's longest continuously operating brewpub. "I watched what they were doing, asked questions, even worked for a while at the bar, learning all I could about beer and brewing. Then I bought an all-grain kit and made a cream ale that my friends really liked."

He'd brewed his first batch of beer in 2008 and, within a few years, discovered that he wanted to turn his hobby turned passion into a professional job. He wanted to own a brewpub. At first, he tried to buy Eske's, but it wasn't available. Then he realized that with its four-season tourist industry, Taos could certainly support a second brewpub. In 2011, he found the ideal spot

Located just north of the center of town, Taos Ale House offers beers brewed in house, along with a number of other New Mexico craft beers. *Courtesy the author.*

for a brewpub on Paseo Pueblo del Norte, the main street through town. The building, which had been an auto mechanics depot and, most recently, an art gallery, was within walking distance of galleries, shops and motels.

Using his woodworking skills, Cook, with the help of friends who'd enjoyed his home-brew, began to transform the space. They beamed the ceiling with vigas, installed a hardwood floor, built a kiva fireplace in one corner and installed a one-and-a-half-barrel brewing system. Cook added a pool table, shuffleboard and two televisions. On the walls, he displayed art and photography by local artists. Outside the front entrance, a bricked patio provided a space where patrons could enjoy the warm summer nights and spring and autumn days. When it opened in 2011, the brewery offered simple meals in the small kitchen. Then Cook leased the kitchen to Gringo Taco. In the summer of 2014, he will be partnering with a successful Kansas hamburger restaurant, the Hamburger Stand.

When he was in San Diego, Cook discovered that he liked big IPAs, porters and stouts. During the first few months Taos Ale house was open, he offered more than twenty different styles. "Now that I've found what people like best and what I can brew with consistency, I'm limiting myself." Not surprisingly, these styles include some "big beers." But Cook emphasized, "Even though my beers are big, they don't seem too high in alcohol." The champion is Mogul IPA, a 9.5 percent ABV, 100 IBU ale that uses Chinook and Golding hops. It is closely followed by Curcurbita Imperial Ale, an 8.7 percent ABV pumpkin beer. Lower-alcohol styles include La Rubia, a blonde ale with a gentle malt profile and nonthreatening hop finish designed as an entry-level beer; the Simple Porter (6.3 percent ABV), a fairly dry, medium-bodied drink with smoky and understated chocolate notes; and a dunkelweizen.

Taos Ale House has proved popular with locals and with tourists who have wandered up from town or are returning from Taos Pueblo or, in the winter, the ski slopes. One of the most interesting locals is a high school teacher who sits at a table, spreads out his papers, orders a pint and begins grading. There is no report on how the grades he awards are influenced by his choice of one of the big beers or one of the lower-alcohol varieties.

TAOS MESA BREWING

20 ABC Mesa Road, El Prado, 87529
575-758-1900, www.taosmesabrewing.com
Taproom: At the brewery.

Many of the buildings that house New Mexico microbreweries and brewpubs have interesting histories: one began as New Mexico's Ford dealership, another was the home of a late nineteenth-century butcher shop and another was a twenty- by twenty-foot log cabin that housed a farm's blacksmith shop. But the home of Taos Mesa Brewing has a very short history: it's a brand-new Quonset hut. However, the building and its creators are stories in themselves.

The idea for the brewpub was born five years before the place opened for business in July 2012. Four men wanted to build a place where locals and tourists alike could listen to good music, eat good food, drink good beer and gaze at magnificent scenery. Peter Kolshorn was an architect who specialized

Located in an industrial area northwest of Taos, Taos Mesa Brewing is housed in an imaginatively designed Quonset hut. *Courtesy the author.*

in sustainable buildings. Dan Irion was a restaurateur who was active in the local band scene. Gary Feuerman was a lawyer and businessman. Jayson Wylie was a onetime home-brewer who, Kolshorn said, has "the passion, scientific knowledge and expertise" necessary to make good beer.

The next step involved choosing a location. The one they selected seemed very unpromising, but it wasn't too expensive. It was located ten miles outside Taos in El Prado, on the north side of U.S. Highway 64 in an industrial area that has many buildings and yards for which the term "eyesore" would be kindly. Unless you were dropping off passengers at the airport or you worked there, the location was hardly a destination. Tourists would drive through on the way to view the spectacular Rio Grande Gorge or on longer trips to northern New Mexico and southern Colorado.

As the building to house their new enterprise, they chose a Quonset hut, that plainest and most utilitarian of structures. But when Taos Mesa Brewing opened, visitors discovered that the building was like no other Quonset hut they'd ever seen. The entire south side is covered with solar collectors to supply heat for the building and for preheating of the brewing water; the north side is insulated by lightweight pumice concrete. Across the west end of the building is a large stage, behind which is the brewery. Large glass windows fill nearly all the east end, looking out onto the beer garden, volleyball court, two music amphitheaters and, beyond that, the Sangre de Cristo Mountains. The Taos Mesa building and grounds are, as one of the partners suggested, "an oasis in an industrial wasteland."

In finishing the building, old materials were reclaimed, refurbished and reused. Old CD shelves from a Santa Fe record store became sconces for the side lighting; the large overhead lights had seen earlier duty in an old school gymnasium. The sound baffles around the stage are large pieces of recycled rubber cut to resemble ravens' wings, which are part of the brewpub's logo. Tables and chairs, all salvaged and reconditioned, surround a hardwood dance floor in front of the stage. On Sunday mornings, before the building is opened for its specialty brunch, members of the local women's roller derby team push chairs and tables to the walls and skate on the concrete, circling the edge of the dance floor. Kolshorn scrounged pieces of broken glass, fossils and bike gears and set them into concrete, which was then buffed and made into the bar.

Behind the bar, a small door opens to a chute, down which is rolled the food that is prepared in a renovated food truck parked a few feet from the north wall. The food includes such pub favorites as chips and salsa, pretzels and green chile cheeseburgers, along with a Maryland crab cake sandwich and a portobello sandwich. Apple and plum pies baked at nearby Taos Pueblo are also served. The mimosa brunch includes Mexican rice cereal, lamb loin and blue cheese chiliquiles and green curry pork and eggs.

Head Brewer Jayson Wylie was an admitted Bud and Coors Lite drinker until an army buddy introduced him to German lagers. "That's when I discovered that you could really have an experience with beer. I was amazed by the variety styles and how they all tasted good." He became a home-brewer, a hobby he continued when he moved from his home in Kansas to Taos. It was when he was working as a bartender at Eske's in downtown Taos that he really considered turning a hobby into a profession. "I watched what Eske and [Head Brewer] Chris Jones were doing, I asked questions and I learned so much." Ironically, Jones is now working for Wylie, having moved from Eske's in the summer of 2013.

For Jayson, making beer in Taos is both a delight and a challenge. "Albuquerque is the only city or town in New Mexico where the people drink more craft beer than here. The residents have a very sophisticated palate. And so do a lot of the tourists who come to Taos; they like to visit the local microbreweries. Peter told me that on the day we opened, a group of guys who'd come to ski came into the brewpub. They'd seen the small sign on the road and told him that they stopped at local breweries wherever they went."

"When I started home-brewing, I liked hops, and I upped the bitterness levels as much as I could. But I've changed. Here we want to have sessionable beers; if something's too hoppy, you really can't taste much after the first couple of beers. And we want to offer a variety of styles, from a lighter kolsch-style beer to a dark porter. We have several guest taps so that people can experience the great range of New Mexico beers."

Kolsch 45 can be both an entry-level beverage for craft beer novices and an interesting interpretation of a classic German style for beer aficionados. The 4.8 percent ABV ale is light-bodied and crisp and presents a subtle variety of hop and malt flavors. Lunch Pale Ale is a 5.2 percent ABV English-style beer that uses Golding hops to provide both a mild bitterness and an earthiness that complement the malts. Hopper (named after the actor Dennis) IPA is in the West Coast style and uses Cascade, Columbus, Chinook and Centennial hops. Crisp, dry and citrusy, it is a strong beer at 6.2 percent and, at 75 IBUs, the hoppiest of Taos Mesa's offerings.

Fall Down Brown is in the tradition of an English session ale. It's a 4.6 pecent ABV beer, with a light roastiness in the malt flavors. Wylie compared it to that popular British brand Newcastle Brown. Notorious ESB (4.8 percent ABV) is also based on a favorite English style, one in which the malt flavors are complemented more aggressively with hops that provide piney and spicy notes. Superstitious Stout (5.2 percent ABV) is a creamy oatmeal stout with smoky, roasted and chocolate notes, somewhat like the famous Guinness.

Within a few months of its opening, Taos Mesa Brewing had become extremely popular—even beyond the imaginings of its optimistic founders. People were flocking to the "oasis" in the Industrial Park desert of El Prado to enjoy the building, the view, the activities, the music, the food and the beer. Already, the brewery has been expanded.

As he surveyed the crowd one evening, Peter Kolshorn remembered the planning stages of the venture and laughed. "We'd put together a very sound business plan, but none of the banks was interested. So we went out and rounded up our own investors. Now our investors are making money, and the banks aren't getting any interest."

CHAPTER 7
NORTHERN NEW MEXICO

ABBEY BREWING COMPANY

1305 Forest Service Road, #151, Abiquiu, 87510
505-670-6802, www.christdesert.org/Abbey_Beverage_Company
Taproom: Bode's General Store, 21196 U.S. Highway 84, Abiquiu.

The brewing traditions of Belgium extend back to the Middle Ages, when most monasteries made their own beer. However, it wasn't until the 1990s, with the establishment of New Belgium in Fort Collins; Brewery Ommegang in Cooperstown, New York; and Celis Brewery in Austin, Texas, that styles from this centuries-old tradition attracted the attention of craft brew drinkers. And it wasn't until 2005 that Abbey Brewing Company, the first American monastery brewery since before the Prohibition era, began operations.

The new brewing company was a joint venture of two New Mexico Benedictine monasteries: Our Lady of Guadalupe, in Pecos, and Monastery of Christ in the Desert, just outside Abiquiu. The brewing operation began as a means of raising funds to be used in meeting the monasteries' operating expenses and charitable work. Creating quality beer fit into the order's mission "to bring everything to perfection for the glory of God." This goal was reflected in the new brewery's slogan: "Made with care and prayer."

Abbey Brewing's first and only head brewer, Brad Kraus, a pioneer and two-decade veteran of the New Mexico craft beer movement, set up a small brewing system at the Pecos site; bottling operations took place at the newly opened Sierra Blanca brewing facility in Moriarty. As orders for Monks' Ale, the first offering, increased, most of the brewing was shifted to Moriarty. By the end of the first decade of the century, the Pecos monastery's interest in the brewery had diminished greatly, and the Monastery of Christ in the Desert bought out its interest.

In 2006, Abbey Brewing produced 127 barrels of Monks' Ale, which was available in bottle and draft, mainly in New Mexico. Since then, distribution has expanded into Pennsylvania and across the south and west from Louisiana to California. In 2013, production reached 1,400 barrels annually. In 2010, a second beer, Monks' Wit appeared. Monks' Tripel and Monks' Dubbel were released in 2012 and 2013, respectively.

Reaching the headquarters of Abbey Brewing, located on the grounds of Monastery of Christ in the Desert, requires a drive through some of New Mexico's most spectacular scenery: northeast out of the town of Abiquiu along Highway 84 and then thirteen miles along Forest Service Road 51, a winding gravel road that follows the Chama River Valley.

The abbey itself, built in 1964, seems to grow out of the cliffs that tower behind it and, indeed, strives to be part of the living landscape. On the way to the pilot brewery, which is some two or three hundred yards from the monastery, visitors pass a half-acre field in which several varieties of native New Mexico hops, for use in experimental brews, are planted. The road continues past a field of solar collectors used to generate electricity for the monastery and outbuildings and comes to a stop near what could be mistaken for a large shed or garage. It is the pilot brewery and houses equipment from Pecos and, since 2012, the taproom, where beer lovers who have made the long drive from the main highway sample and buy the brews. It is here that the tripel and dubbel were developed. As soon as possible, the brewery will be expanded to enable all of the brewing of special, limited-addition beers to take place here.

Four people oversee the brewing and business operations of Abbey Brewing: Head Brewer Brad Kraus; Business Manager Berkeley Merchant; Abbey Cellarer Brother Christian Leisy; and Rich Weber, principal owner of the Sierra Blanca brewing complex in Moriarty.

Kraus, a New Mexico native who had earned a degree in chemistry at Houston's Rice University, returned to his home state when the Land of Enchantment's microbrewing movement was in its infancy. His résumé included startup work for Rio Bravo, Wolf Canyon and Isotopes Brewing Companies, as well as for brewers in Columbia and Chile. The depth of his brewing experience, along with the variety of breweries with which he has worked, enabled him to develop recipes that fitted in with the abbey tradition that the monks wanted to revive and to act as a mentor and teacher to the monks and Merchant, the general manager.

Merchant, who had moved to Santa Fe from Portland, Oregon, to retire from his work as a startup consultant for tech businesses, began a new career when the abbott of Christ in the Desert asked if he would become the general manager of the brewery, which in 2009 was about to begin a new growth phase. Merchant had been a home-brewer in college, and one of his first full-time jobs was with a company that did work for Strohs, the legendary Detroit brewery. "I had the run of the whole brewery when I was in Detroit, and I learned a lot about the science, art and engineering of brewing. Since I've come here, my passion for making beer has grown. I read, [and] I learn everything I can about brewing. Brad Kraus has been a great teacher." Merchant takes an active role in sales, especially in markets beyond the home area of New Mexico, visiting distributors and attending beer festivals.

Brother Christian Leisy oversees the work of other monks who are involved in the sourcing of materials and, frequently, in the brewing and bottling processes, both at the monastery and in Moriarty. When he discussed the hop yard that had been planted, he recalled a youthful experience with one of beer's essential ingredients. "When I was a young monk, one of my jobs was taking part in the hop harvest in California. The smell was so powerful that you couldn't get it out of your clothes; when the season was finished, you just threw them away."

In addition to the work that takes place around the monastery and the brewery, Leisy also travels with Berkeley Merchant to festivals in areas where the beer is distributed. "At first, he was a novelty," Merchant remembered. "Here was a tall man dressed in a long, dark, hooded robe, providing samples of our beer to festivalgoers." Leisy remembered that people often asked him if he drank the beer himself, and he explained that the brothers enjoyed it on special occasions—but in moderation.

Rich Weber—who built the brewery in Moriarty to be a place where several brewers could cut costs by sharing equipment and space—works cooperatively with Merchant, Kraus and Leisy during the creation of the various Monks' ales. "He doesn't contract-brew for us," Merchant emphasized. "We oversee all aspects of the brewing process, and we own a

Abbey Beverage's brewing operations are overseen by Berkeley Merchant (left) and Brother Christian Leisy. *Courtesy the author.*

fermenter and a bright tank. We're responsible for the final product, but he helps us to make sure it's the best it can be."

Monks' Ale, Abbey Brewing's first and its flagship beer, is designated on the brewery's website as an Abbey Single (Enkel) Ale, which is darker than but similar to a Belgian pale ale. A 5.2 percent ABV beer, it is amber/copper in color and pours with a light tan head. It is a medium-bodied brew in which malt flavors dominate, although the Belgian yeasts provide both fruity and spicy notes. When it first came out, some drinkers, familiar with New Belgium's Fat Tire Ale, commented that Monks' was like that Colorado brew, but with more pronounced flavors. As the brewery's initial offering, it was different enough from other beers to be distinctive but not so unusual as to be threatening.

Having succeeded with Monks' Ale, it was only natural for Abbey Brewing to offer what has become the most popular of all Belgian styles, a wit (or white) wheat beer. "This is where Brad Kraus's experience as a brewer was so important," Berkeley Merchant remarked, explaining that, while in

Texas, Brad had come to know expatriate Belgian brewer Pierre Celis, who was renowned for having revived the almost forgotten wit beer style. "Brad insisted that we had to use Indian coriander and the peel of sweet Spanish oranges along with a secret ingredient. That's what gives our version its distinctive style," Merchant noted. Straw colored, with the style's distinctive haze, the fruit and spice notes do not overwhelm the malts.

Merchant and Kraus created Abbey Brewing's limited-release beers, a 9.2 percent ABV Belgian tripel and a 6.7 percent ABV dubbel. The tripel, which uses the monastery's hops, pours what one taster called "a beautiful gold color." The fruity and earthy aromas give way on first sips to tastes resembling apricot, peach and plum. Light to medium-bodied, it has a gentle effervescence, and as the beverage warms slightly in the glass, the taste of the alcohol contributes to but does not overwhelm the other flavors. The dubbel is bronze in color. A smooth, medium-bodied beer, it has a rich, sweet maltiness, with a plum finish.

Having established their skills at creating ales based on a revered Belgian tradition, Berkeley Merchant and Brother Christian Leisy are looking to the future by researching another historical tradition. In the fall of 2013, they traveled to Germany. "The Abbey tradition isn't limited to Belgium," Merchant explained. "We want to learn more about what other monasteries created. We want to find out if we can successfully continue their traditions here at the Abbey of Christ in the Desert."

BLUE HERON BREWING COMPANY

2214 Highway 68, Embudo, 87531
505-579-9188, www.blueheronbrews.com
Taproom: At the brewery.

Every morning, after her children had been picked up by the school bus in Rinconada, a small village twenty minutes south of Taos, Kristin Hennelly would walk back to her house at the edge of the Rio Grande, pausing to look at the small, one-story building beside New Mexico Highway 68 and then to fantasize. The building, which had been a home, a gas station, a grocery store and an art gallery, was now vacant. Kristin thought it would be a perfect location for the brewpub she'd dreamed of opening.

Located a few hundred feet from the Rio Grande, Blue Heron Brewing is a popular stop for tourists on their way to and from Taos. *Courtesy the author.*

She'd grown up in the nearby village of Dixon, where her father and uncle were winemakers and where a close family friend, Brandon Santos, had been the brewer for the nearby Embudo Station Brewpub. However, it wasn't until she was attending the University of Montana and had met her future husband, Scott, a home-brewer, that she became interested in brewing. "We returned here when Scott was hired at the National Lab in Los Alamos. "When I decided to open the brewpub, he and Brandon taught me about brewing, and together we developed a number of recipes."

The little building had space for a three-barrel brewing system, a bar and a few tables. The backyard would make an ideal warm-weather patio. It was at the edge of a highway well traveled by tourists, large numbers of whom stopped to take river-rafting excursions that ended nearby. Blue Heron Brewing Company opened in 2010. "I decided to name the brewery after the birds because, when I looked out my window, I could see them wading in the river."

"I wanted to give the beers interesting names, something that people would remember. A lot of the names are Spanish, as a tribute to what was the dominant language around here for generations," said Kristin. Embudo Gold, Oro de Rio Grande and Penasco Porter refer to nearby places; La Llorona

Bosque Brewing Company's emblem is a leaf from the cottonwood tree, which is found in most of the wooded areas bordering New Mexico rivers. *Courtesy Bosque Brewing.*

As part of its marketing strategy, Tractor redesigned the labels for Farmer's Tan, its bestselling ale, replacing the cartoon-like drawing with a more stylized image. *Courtesy the author.*

Established in 1994, Il Vicino is the third-oldest operating brewery in New Mexico. *Courtesy Il Vicino Brewing Company.*

The name La Cumbre means "the peak" (as in mountain) and indicates both the mountainous terrain of New Mexico and the high level of brewing quality sought by owner Jeff Erway and his brewers. *Courtesy LaCumbre Brewing Company.*

Like many breweries, Nexus has created a slogan that plays with the word for its principal product. *Courtesy Nexus Brewery.*

A Georgia O'Keeffe–style buffalo skull and a Dia de los Muertos skull are found on the labels of two of Sierra Blanca's most popular beers. *Courtesy Sierra Blanca Brewing Company.*

CHICKEN KILLER
Barley Wine Ale

new mexico's first microbrewery

Santa Fe Brewing Company

Depicted on the label of Chicken Killer Barley Wine Ale is the dachshund that ran amok in Santa Fe Brewing founder Mike Levis's barnyard.

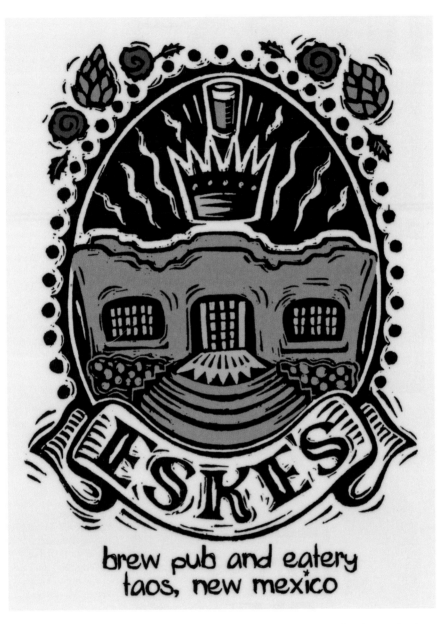

Eske's, New Mexico's oldest continuously operating brewpub, is located in what used to be the family home of a prominent Taos family. *Courtesy the author.*

Top: The four founders and co-owners of Taos Mesa Brewing are (left to right) Dan Irion, Gary Feuerman, Peter Kolshorn and Jayson Wylie. *Courtesy the author.*

Bottom: Monks' Ales are produced by Abbey Beverage Company, the first American monastery brewery since the Prohibition era. *Courtesy Abbey Beverage.*

Opposite, top: Brewer Peter Fieweger (right) and his assistant Brandon Beard in the cramped quarters of the brew house. *Courtesy the author.*

Opposite, bottom: High Desert Brewing Company is the only one of three 1990s Las Cruces brewpubs that is still operational. *Courtesy the author.*

MONKS' ALE®

made with care and prayer®

Abbey Beverage Company, LLC

Opposite, top: Roosevelt Brewing is the first craft brewery to be opened in eastern New Mexico. *Courtesy Roosevelt Brewing.*

Opposite, bottom: The New Mexico Zia sun emblem is displayed prominently on bottles and cans from Santa Fe Brewing Company. *Courtesy Santa Fe Brewing.*

Top: The raven is the emblem of Taos Mesa Brewing Company, one of the state's newer brewpubs. *Courtesy Taos Mesa Brewing.*

Bottom: Located in Farmington, Three Rivers Eatery & Brewery features an image of Shiprock, the famous nearby landmark, on one of its labels. *Courtesy Three Rivers Eatery & Brewery.*

La Cumbre Brewing Company's slogans and beer names reflect owner Jeff Erway's love of New Mexico's mountain scenery. *Courtesy the author.*

In front of Tractor Brewing Company's original home in Los Lunas stands one of the many dozen farm vehicles, full sized and miniature, that owner Herb Pleumer has collected. *Courtesy the author.*

Top: A pint glass awaits filling with one of Bosque Brewing Company's ales. *Courtesy Clare Stott.*

Bottom: Mateo Lowther (left) and Bob Gosselin are head brewer and owner, respectively, of High Desert Brewing Company of Las Cruces. *Courtesy the author.*

Donavan Lane, brewer and co-owner of Broken Bottle Brewery, executes the not-so-easy task of filling a growler. *Courtesy the author.*

Il Vicino's Brady McKeown (center), one of New Mexico's longest-serving head brewers, is surrounded by members of his "Brew Crew." *Courtesy the author.*

Head Brewer Daniel Jaramillo (left) and owner Jeff Erway check supplies in La Cumbre's brew house. *Courtesy the author.*

Brewer Mike Campbell inspects a glass of beer that he has newly brewed for Las Cazuela's of Rio Rancho. *Courtesy the author.*

Head Brewer Mark Matheson (left) and owner Nico Ortiz of Turtle Mountain Brewing in Rio Rancho. *Courtesy the author.*

Roosevelt Brewing owner Justin Cole pours a pint at the brewpub in Portales. *Courtesy the author.*

Award-winning brewer John Bullard stands beside the oak barrels in which are aging special beers that he has created for Santa Fe's Blue Corn Brewery. *Courtesy the author.*

Trent Edwards, owner of Duel Brewing, Santa Fe's newest brewpub, stands in front of a piece of antique furniture that was turned into a serving counter. Flanking him are General Manager Matt Onstott (left) and brewer Todd Yocham. *Courtesy the author.*

The cofounders of Marble Brewery—brewer Ted Rice (left), Director of Operations John Gozigian (center) and President Jeff Jinnett (right)—stand in front of shelves containing Rice's extensive beer can collection. *Courtesy the author.*

Illinois Brewery of Socorro, built in the late nineteenth century, is now home to the Hammel Museum of the Socorro Historical Society. *Courtesy the author.*

Scottish Ale celebrates a famous character in New Mexico folklore; and Tarantula Trek is named after a spider she saw dancing across her front yard.

"I knew that we'd have a lot of tourists with different experiences of beer and a taste for different styles, so we decided to offer a range of styles from light to dark." Fourteen beers are offered on a rotating basis: nine ales, three lagers and two seasonals. Six are on tap at one time; four are available in twenty-two-ounce bottles.

Embudo Gold Golden Ale and Tarantula Trek Red Ale are designed as entry-level beers. The former is a lower-alcohol ale that, when they are available, uses local Cascade hops grown by Kristin's cousin. The latter she describes as malty, well balanced and a little sweeter than the golden ale. Amber's Folly Amber Ale, described on the website as "a typical American Amber Ale with a malty caramel background," and Lava Rock Pale Ale emphasize a balance between the hops and malts. Cascabel IPA is, Kristin emphasized, "definitely not a hop bomb. It has earthy undertones that make it more like an English IPA."

La Llorona Scottish Ale is Blue Heron's most popular beer. "I did a lot of research on Scottish ales and then developed my own recipe," she noted. Smooth and dark, it has chocolate notes and is drier than many interpretations of the style. Penasco Porter and Prieta Real Imperial Stout complete the dark side of Blue Heron's offerings.

Unfortunately, the brewpub's three lagers are usually only available in the cooler months. "We just don't have the cool lagering space for them in the summer." Kristin explained. Oro de Rio Grande Pilsner is in a Czech style, while XXX Maibock is a light bock. La Cabra (a female goat) Doppel Bock is described as a "dark, creamy bock with a hint of chocolate, slightly hopped." Autumn Sun is a light ale that uses local hops, and Los Duraznos Peach Ale is the only flavored beer offered.

COMANCHE CREEK BREWING COMPANY

225 Comanche Creek Road, Eagle Nest, 87718
575-377-2337, www.comanchecreekbrewingco.com
Taproom: At the brewery.

Just north of Eagle Nest, a very small sign at the edge of Highway 38 points in the direction of Comanche Creek Brewing Company. A gravel road

Comanche Creek Brewing Company's owner/brewer Koby Mutz stands beside the onetime blacksmith shop that now serves as a brew house. *Courtesy the author.*

winds eastward and upward toward the tree line of the Sangre de Cristo Mountains, ending at what looks like a small log cabin. Near the log cabin stands an old harvester with iron wheels. Early in the morning, deer, elk, coyotes, wild turkeys and occasionally a black bear wander in the space between the twenty- by twenty-foot building and Comanche Creek.

There are signs that this is more than just an old building in what used to be a farmer's field. Behind the log cabin is a plastic-walled Port-A-Potty; in front, just outside the only door, there are benches hewn from logs and a chiminea. Just inside the door stand the mash tun and kettle of a three-barrel brewing system. The log cabin, which had been built more than seventy years ago to house a blacksmith shop, is the home of Comanche Creek Brewing, and the benches are part of what is called the "Biergarten," the spot where locals and tourists can sit; enjoy the magnificent scenery; breathe in the crisp, clean mountain air; and sip on a pint of ale brewed by Koby Mutz, the establishment's owner, brewer and, along with his wife, Tasha, one of the 1.5 employees.

Comanche Creek Brewing Company, established in 2010 by the husband-and-wife team, is, at four hundred square feet, one of the smallest breweries and has one of the smallest annual productions—twenty-five barrels in

2012—in the United States. Situated at an altitude of eight thousand feet, it is certainly one of the most "elevated." Mutz noted that the altitude created some problems: the boil was longer, carbonation was a little difficult and fermentation took longer and was more finicky.

The Mutzes had lived in Denver, where he was a commercial real estate broker and she a nurse. Fans of Colorado's rich and varied craft brewing culture, they had become home-brewers, testing recipes in the kitchen of their condo. When the real estate business went south late in 2009, Kody decided to head south, literally—back to the family homestead outside Eagle Nest, specifically to the log cabin. "I thought that it would be a great opportunity to turn my hobby into a profession. I'd long been inspired by the story of how Kim Jordan and Jeff Lebesch had founded New Belgium Brewing Company in their garage." The log cabin wasn't any bigger than a garage, but it was located in a spectacularly beautiful valley that attracted an increasingly large number of winter and summer tourists.

As he developed his recipes, he had to keep in mind the clientele he would be serving. "Rural people have been slower to join the craft beer movement," he remarked. "I knew that the higher alcohol and very hoppy bears that are so popular in the Northwest and in Colorado wouldn't be as well received here. That was also true for a large number of our winter and summer visitors who come from Kansas and Texas. I needed to create beers that were very approachable and easy drinking. I'd also have to keep the alcohol content lower so that people who visited our biergarten would be able to drive safely back to their homes or the motels in town."

Homestead Amber, Comanche Creek's flagship beer, is based on an alt bier recipe that Mutz developed as a home-brewer. A medium-bodied beverage with chocolate and caramel notes, it has a slight hop finish. It is 5.5 percent alcohol by volume and a low 15 IBUs. "It's an easy crossover," Mutz noted. "People don't find the flavor overpowering."

He also brews four lighter ales and two darker ones, along with a pale and a double IPA. Kolsch, Creek Side Blonde and Gold Rush Golden Ale are definitely designed as crossover beers, being neither too strong nor too hoppy. Old Smoky, a *rauch* beer built on an Irish Red base, and Iron Mountain Porter use darker malts but remain around 5 percent ABV. Dead Man Pale Ale and Touch-Me-Not IPA (named after a mountain on the east side of the valley) are malty in the English style, although the IPA does use the Cascade and Chinook hops popular in West Coast IPAs.

New Mexico Craft Brewing Company

1212 Railroad Avenue, Las Vegas, 87701
505-426-6079
Taproom: The Old Town Draft House, 139 Bridge Street, Las Vegas.

The story of the founding of New Mexico Craft Brewing Company is a familiar one, but with a twist. Albuquerque home-brewer Miguel Melendez and two of his buddies decided that they should start a microbrewery. "I had a business that I operated in Las Vegas and thought it might be an idea to open a brewery there." The choice of the small northern New Mexican town was helped by the fact that they applied for and received a grant from the Highlands University Foundation Grant, affiliated with the local state university. "They wanted to support someone who would be a catalyst to spark business in Las Vegas and so forge a link with the local university."

Miguel and his friends purchased a fifteen-barrel brew house that had belonged to Milagro Brewery of Bernalillo before it went out of business in 2005, acquired a small warehouse near the edge of town and applied for a small brewers license. When the equipment had been assembled and the license approved, they planned to set about brewing beer.

However, they hadn't counted on three local residents, former students of Highlands, who had seen the application and presented themselves as the people who could create beers for the new company. "We immediately saw that they were better equipped to do the job than we were and hired them," Melendez remembered." In addition to being former home-brewers, the new crew—Joshua Woodlee, Ben Remmers and Kyle Yonan—were also artists, bringing a mix of science and creativity to the work. Yonan also had a degree in microbiology and was able to apply his scientific knowledge to the production of the beers. The brewery began producing and selling beer in the fall of 2012.

Because of the range of beer-drinking experiences and tastes in Las Vegas, Melendez decided that New Mexico Craft Brewing should offer a wide array of styles, ranging from a golden ale to a stout. "One of the ways we attracted the people who were used to drinking Bud and Coors was to acquire exclusive beer rights for the local professional baseball team, the Las Vegas Train Robbers. We even converted some of the fans to our stout," Melendez remembered. But he went on to add that, even though many of the locals were not used to the bigger, hoppier beers, there was a surprisingly large contingent

New Mexico Craft Brewing Company is the first brewery in Las Vegas since before Prohibition days. *Courtesy New Mexico Craft Brewing.*

of craft beer drinkers: faculty and students at Highlands University, as well as faculty (and sometimes students) at the Armand Hammer World College, an international school located in the nearby village of Montezuma.

Joshua Woodlee, who is the head brewer, used to drink standard mass-market beers. "Then, in the mid-1990s, my mother bought me a beer-brewing kit. After I'd used it, I bought Charlie Papazian's *The Joy of Home Brewing*, and I was hooked."

"I like robust beers," Woodlee said. "But Kyle likes hoppy beers, so we make sure we have some of both." He went on to describe the range of beers, noting that many of them are American interpretations of well-known British styles. Among the brewery's offerings are a simply named Pilsner (Bohemian style), Cerveza de Vapor (a California common or "steam beer"), Starvation Peak "Indian" Pale Ale, Round House Oatmeal Stout, Ojo Rojo (a red ale), Foreign Extra Stout, Silvacide Rye PA (named after a legendary local outlaw), Pantyshot Porter and Tooth Puller Barley Wine.

Until the fifteen-barrel system was refurbished and set up, the brewing was done on a one-half-barrel system that Joshua had concocted when he was a home-brewer. Accordingly, production was small, and New Mexico Craft Brewing beers are found in limited places. "We're focusing on the northeastern part of the state," Melendez said. "We have a taproom in Las Vegas, the Old Town Draft House and taps in Angel Fire, Taos, Santa Fe and Española. As we expand, we'll move into the Albuquerque area."

THREE RIVERS EATERY & BREWERY

101 East Main Street, Farmington, 87401
505-324-2187, www.threeriversbrewery.com
Taproom: At the brewery.

In the mid-1990s, Bob and Cindy Beckley, along with partner John Silva, bought the nearly ninety-year-old Andrews Building at the corner of Main and Orchard Streets in Farmington. Once the home of the Farmington Drugstore and the *Farmington Times-Hustler* newspaper, it was now part of a downtown that was virtually dead. Many storefronts were boarded up, and when the businesses that were operating closed up for the day, the area was basically deserted.

"We paid $60,000 for the property," Beckley remembered. "At first we rented parts of it out, but we wanted to start our own business. I'd done some research about other smaller cities with dying downtowns and found that two types of businesses could succeed: bakeries with attached coffee shops and brewpubs. I'd worked in a bakery before, and I certainly didn't want to get up at two o'clock every morning. John and Cindy agreed, so we settled on a brewpub."

People thought that the trio was crazy, opening a brewpub in a Budweiser town, establishing it in a moribund location and making it a no-smoking premises. Bankers weren't too impressed either, and after two years and twenty rejections from banks, Silva and the Beckleys turned to friends, family and the Small Business Association. They even offered the stainless steel brewing equipment as security to one friend. "We told him that if things didn't work out, he could sell the metal and get back more money than he invested."

"Now we had to turn the old building into a restaurant/brewpub and find a brewer," Beckley remembered. "We refinished the hardwood flooring and repainted the gilt and silver tin ceiling tiles and deepened the basement by hand, carrying out the rocks one at a time. John and I tossed a coin to decide who would learn how to brew. I lost but discovered a great passion: making beer. My friend Bill Carver, who owned a brewpub in Durango, Colorado, taught me how to brew and helped me to set up our brew house."

Three Rivers Brewery, named after the San Juan, Animas and La Plata Rivers that converge in the area, opened in 1997. The Beckleys and Silva were a little anxious. Would their customers accept styles different from what nearly everyone in town was used to? They needn't have been anxious. "It didn't take long for there to be lineups to get in."

Three Rivers is an important part of Farmington's revitalized downtown. *Courtesy the author.*

It was after the tragic events of September 11, 2001, that Bob Beckley realized that Three Rivers had become an important part not only of downtown but also of the larger Farmington community. "We debated on whether we should open or not. And as soon as we did open, the place filled up very quickly, and it stayed that way all day and night. People saw our brewpub as a place to gather as a community, to grieve and to try to understand what had happened."

Within a few years, Three Rivers began an expansion program that involved acquiring and renovating three adjacent buildings. The first step was to expand the overcrowded restaurant into what was a more modern building next door. Then the owners created a pizzeria and a banquet hall and finally acquired another historic building, which they converted into a taproom and game room. "We realized that a separate taproom, away from the family atmosphere of the restaurant, would be best."

The taproom contains six pool tables, shuffleboard, a dartboard and a hopscotch game painted on the floor. In its squares are the names of the various Three Rivers beers. On the windows of the taproom and the restaurant, signs announce that both places constitute a "Husband Day Care Center." The signs go on to ask three questions: "Need time to relax? Need time to yourself? Want to go shopping?" They then suggest a solution: "Leave your husband with us! We'll look after him for you! You only pay for food, drinks, and tip! Husbands must be picked up before closing." Displayed along the walls in both the restaurant and the taproom are items from what is reported to be the world's largest collection of beer labels—more than six thousand, with no duplicates.

The restaurant building possesses something very unusual: a resident ghost that is reported to be the spirit of a woman who died in the apartments above what was then the drugstore. "She comes and goes," Bob Beckley said, "and she seems to be harmless. She was particularly active when we first opened and would occasionally play tricks on customers. One day, four ladies who were sitting in a booth began to shriek. There were four water glasses on the table, and she was rotating them around."

The food menu features New Mexico pub grub: chile cheese fries, green chile stew, Albuquerque turkey sandwiches (made from whole turkeys processed in the kitchen) and pork belly Cubano sandwiches. The pizzeria offers subs, calzones and, of course, pizzas, the dough for which is made daily on the premises. The food may be washed down with root beer made in house, the house beers and even Budweiser. "We respect everyone's taste and preference," Beckley explained, although he admitted that he does want to educate his patrons about craft beer.

The making of the beer is the responsibility of Peter Fieweger and Brandon Beard. Head Brewer Fieweger, a Connecticut native, had become a home-brewer by the time he moved to New Mexico in the 1990s. His first professional job was with Milagro Brewery and Restaurant, a high-end establishment in Bernalillo. "The head brewer had no experience as a brewer, so even though I was technically his assistant, I handled most of the brewing duties." After Milagro went out of business, Fieweger moved to Farmington, working as an assistant brewer at Three Rivers until 2011. Beard, his assistant, a native Farmingtonian, began work as dishwasher at the restaurant, became kitchen manager and then chef before transferring to the brew house. A true craft beer aficionado, he plans his vacation travels around visits to microbreweries. For one of his birthdays, he made a special trip to the Bruery in Los Angeles to sample its sour and barrel-aged beers. When Fieweger retires in 2014, Beard will take over as head brewer.

Because Three Rivers always has twelve beers on tap, the two are kept extremely busy in the ten-barrel brew house. "We have a range from light to dark, lower to higher alcohol," Fieweger said. "Something for everyone." Four beers—Papa Bear Golden Honey Ale, Arroyo Amber Ale, an IPA and a Scottish ale, along with Red Apple Flyer Cider—are always on tap.

After a decade and a half, Papa Bear, one of the brewery's first offerings, remains the bestseller. This 5 percent ABV beer, originally designed to be an entry-level, crossover beer for Farmington residents not familiar with craft beers, is a rounded beverage, with subtle honey notes. The originally very unpopular IPA is now, along with the Red Apple Flyer Cider, the number-two seller. In fact, Beard noted, "We can hardly keep up with the demand." The Centennial, Simcoe, Cascade and Citra hops give piney notes, but unlike most American-style IPAs, the bitterness level is fairly low at 60 IBUs. "We didn't want to scare people away," Fieweger explained. Arroyo Amber, a 5 percent ABV beverage, is not as hoppy as most examples of the style and has rich caramel notes. The Scottish ale, 5.9 percent ABV, is a smooth dark amber beer, with complex malt flavors and a slight hop finish.

Of the rotating beers, the kolsch, the Baltic porter and the Bare Naked Aggie Wheat have the most interesting backstories. Kolsch is a delicate, lager-like ale, with generally low alcoholic content. "I made a mistake when I was making a batch by dry-hopping it [adding hops late in the brewing process], but everybody liked it, so we kept doing it that way," Brandon Beard confessed. The Baltic porter is made with lager yeast and is lighter in body and in alcoholic content than its European counterpart. Bare Naked Aggie Wheat Ale is brewed with freshly picked experimental hops from the nearby Navajo Agriculture Products Industries farm.

Bob Beckley hasn't been directly involved in the brewing process since Three Rivers' earlier years. But a decade and a half after the brewpub opened, he maintains his enthusiasm for the beverages his brewers have created. "You know," he remarked, a note of excitement creeping into his voice, "I've had nine careers, and running this brewpub has been the longest. In a brewery, everything is moving and changing. These beers are alive and changing; each one has a name, and each one is different and has its own personality. These beers are almost like pets."

The success of Three Rivers Eatery & Brewery is in many ways a result of the fact that so many visitors to the establishment at Main and Orchard have responded as enthusiastically to these pets as Bob Beckley has.

CHAPTER 8

SOUTHERN NEW MEXICO

DE LA VEGA'S PECAN GRILL AND BREWERY

500 South Telshor Boulevard, Las Cruces, 88011
575-521-1099, www.pecangrill.com
Taproom: At the brewery.

There's no missing De La Vega's Pecan Grill and Brewery. Located at the southeast corner of East Lohan Avenue and South Treshor Boulevard, Las Cruces's busiest intersection, it's at the north end of the Mesilla Valley Mall. A large sign next to the street reads "Brewery," above the pillars on each side of the massive entry doors are the words "Pecan Grill" and on the roof is what looks like an oversized grain silo.

In 2010, when the restaurant then occupying the premises closed, Tom Springer, who had built the place for the now-departed tenants, decided that he would open his own restaurant. "He wanted a restaurant that featured fine dining but was laid back, like the town," said Ashley Springer, Tom's daughter and the restaurant's director of operations. "They decided on an American steakhouse concept. We appeal to families, younger and older couples, university students and business people—a wide range of patrons. We also wanted a restaurant which was similar to those of the higher-end

Although most of its beer is brewed at the Sierra Blanca facility in Moriarty, De La Vega's Pecan Grill recently installed a small brewing system for special, limited-edition beers. *Courtesy the author.*

brewpub chains such as BJs, Gordon Biersch or Rock Bottom. Las Cruces had the size and the demographics for it. But we also wanted it to be local, not just in ownership," Ashley explained.

The name emphasizes the local focus. "Vega" can be loosely translated as "pleasant, fruitful valley or meadow," which the locals are happy to consider a description of the Mesilla Valley in which Las Cruces is set. "Pecan" makes reference to one of New Mexico's major agricultural crops.

For the first three years of operation, the beer wasn't made locally. It was contract-brewed by Sierra Blanca of Moriarty. Seven of De La Vega's regular beers are slightly tweaked versions of Sierra Blanca and Rio Grande styles. For legal reasons, the name of each beer had to be changed. This involved putting *D*s in front of the style name and dropping such recognizable Sierra Blanca names as "Outlaw" and "Alien." In the case of the amber ale, a specifically Las Cruces name was applied: "Aggie," a reference to the New Mexico State University athletic teams.

The most popular beer made for the restaurant-brewpub has been a pecan beer, which adds pecan extract to an amber ale base. "Having the pecan beer has carried us to new levels," Ashley Springer said. "It's our biggest seller in the restaurant, and it's available in bottles all around the state. It's really given us recognition."

In the summer of 2013, De La Vega's acquired its small brewers license and became a brewery in more than just name. A one-barrel pilot system has been installed. Dave Allan, an award-winning home-brewer at the state and national levels, has begun brewing in house. "We are making a test batch each month, seeing what restaurant patrons like," he said. "Our long-term goal is to establish a twenty-barrel production facility in Las Cruces, brewing the beers that have received the most positive responses." Among the test batches that have already been brewed are Vanilla Oak Brown Ale, the Gnome Lord Strong Ale and a Bohemian pilsner. The pilsner, which won Allan gold, silver and bronze medals at New Mexico State Fair competitions, is called "Gelbe Schnee," a German phrase that translates as "yellow snow."

HIGH DESERT BREWING COMPANY

1201 West Hadley Avenue, Las Cruces, 88005
575-525-6752, www.highdesertbrewingco.com
Taproom: At the brewery.

In 1969, when Bob Gosselin, cofounder and owner of High Desert Brewing in Las Cruces, left Massachusetts to study at New Mexico State University, the craft beer movement had not begun. After graduation, he joined the university's Electron Microscope Department, where a co-worker, Mark Cunningham, introduced him to home-brewing. "We won some awards," Bob remembered. "And in the early 1990s, when Santa Fe Brewing started distributing their beers in our area, we thought it might be a good idea to turn our hobby into a profession. Besides, we were getting bored with our regular jobs," he said, laughing.

Gosselin and Cunningham (who died in 2006) had to find a suitable location for and the money to finance their operation. Their brewery had to be in an area that was zoned for both the brewing and on-premises selling of beer and that was in a location that would attract customers. In 1993, they purchased an old adobe brick home that had most recently been used as a secondhand store. Attached to the rear of the small building were two efficiency apartments that would be renovated in later years when High Desert needed to enlarge its brewing operations. Located at the edge of a residential district of modest homes, it was only two blocks from Valley Drive, one of the city's important north–south thoroughfares. It had great potential for what could be called a neighborhood pub.

At a time when banks had not realized what profitable operations brewpubs could be, Gosselin and Cunningham engaged in creative financing. "I had seventeen credit cards, which I used to the max," Gosselin explained. "And when I had to, I sold some of the property I owned." Then, not too long before High Desert's 1997 opening, another problem arose: "The city decided that we had to pave our parking lot. There went another $20,000."

"We were worried. We had a lot invested," Bob remembered. "There was another brewpub in town. Would anybody come to our place? Would they like our beers? Would they come back?" The brewpub broke even its first year, and according to Gosselin, profits have grown steadily since. By the end of their sixth year, the partners had paid off all the debts accrued in the startup process.

High Desert is busy every day, beginning with retired people who come in for a pint with lunch or in the early afternoon, then people on their way home from work and later students and others who come in as the evening wears on—particularly on Thursdays and Saturdays, which are music nights. On warmer evenings, many people sit out on at the covered patio. Inside, many people crowd around the bar, sometimes glancing up at the ceiling from which are hung hundreds of beer coasters contributed by well-traveled customers. Other people sit at tables along walls that at one time were adorned with velvet paintings of Elvis. "Mark thought they were campy." Bob said. On the roof, fifty-three newly installed solar panels power a ten-kilowatt system that provides 20 percent of the brewery's electrical needs.

"Right from the beginning, we've had a core group of people who came here. On most evenings, most of the customers are regulars. We have a lot of cops who dine here; it's out of the way, and they enjoy mixing with other law people. But we've had some unusual visitors," he added. "Once, shortly after the patio was opened, the brewer and one of his friends were sitting on the patio rolling cigarettes. There was a narc sitting at another table. He thought they were rolling a joint, and he called the local police. We got it all straightened out. We never saw him back again. Another time, a visiting rugby team came in after a game at the university. They were the last customers; by the time we closed down, two people were dancing nude on the tables."

Once a secondhand store, this old adobe building was transformed in the 1990s into High Desert Brewing. *Courtesy the author.*

High Desert's motto, "None of our beers suck," was chosen by Cunningham, a fan of the Beavis and Butthead cartoons. "It's a bit brash," Bob remarked, "but it's true. Our beers are very good. We wouldn't have lasted if they weren't." There are close to two dozen styles, with eleven of them always available. "We have a beer that should please just about anyone who comes in." There are three wheat beers, six pale ales, six lagers, six "colored beers" from amber to stout and several relatively rare brews such as kolsch, rye and Scottish. They range in strength from 4 percent ABV for the peach wheat ale to 11 percent ABV for the barley wine.

During High Desert's first decade of operation, Gosselin and Cunningham handled brewing duties. After the latter's death, Matt Valdez took over until 2012, when his assistant, Mateo Lowther became head brewer. "I was your typical Bud drinker," Mateo said, "until my older brother got me to try the craft beers he was drinking. Then he brought me to High Desert. I really took to the hoppy IPAs. I knew I wanted to become a brewer, and for a year, I begged Matt to hire me as an assistant. Finally, he gave in."

Mateo called brewing the most rewarding and demanding job he's ever been in. "The people I brew beer for are only fifty feet away when they drink it. They can be very critical when they don't think a brew is right. But I'm constantly learning, discovering what doesn't work and then learning how to make it work. I'm so hooked that I even home-brew on my days off, trying different techniques and experimenting with different styles."

High Desert makes sure that it has on tap several of what Gosselin called "training beers," the ones that will move people away from the Budweisers and Coors with which they are most familiar and comfortable. "We like to start with the lighter beers and then move them to darker and hoppier ones," Lowther explained. Wheat beer, an American-style brew, and peach wheat, a favorite since the brewpub opened and described as "not for girls only," are lightly hopped 4 percent ABV beers. The next steps are to Bohemian pilsner, a Czech-style lager and Octoberfest. The crisp, light-bodied kolsch serves as an entry into the various colored beers—amber and brown—and the stouts and porters.

Both Gosselin and Lowther discussed the brewery's selection of pale ales with pride. The American Pale Ale strives for a hop-malt balance more in the English style, but the American hops provide citrusy notes. The IPA, which, the description states, "will knock your socks off," is almost completely in the American style. "One of our customers will only drink our IPA. We call him 'IPA Bob,'" Mateo remarked. The Fresh Hopped IPA uses recently harvested hops to impart unique aromas and flavors. "We've been getting our hops from De Smet Farms in central New Mexico," Gosselin noted. "But we've got hop vines growing on the side wall of our brewery, and we hope to be able to use the harvest from them for one or two batches." The Black IPA, the brewery's interpretation of one of the craft brewing industry's newest styles, American black ale, is, the website notes, aggressively hopped and uses generous amounts of roasted malts. About Anniversary Ale, an 8 percent ABV imperial IPA, the website exclaims, "Hopheads rejoice!"

While they sip their beer, patrons may also enjoy the food prepared by the full-service kitchen. The menu, not surprisingly, is southwestern. While there are wings and burgers, Caesar salad and a Reuben sandwich, there are also jalapeño poppers, green chile cheese fries, several types of quesadillas, green chile stew and the house specialty, nachos with black beans, diced tomatoes, jalapeños and salsa, with optional chopped green chile.

There is a television, but only one. In the tradition of a neighborhood pub, most people prefer to talk with one another, or, on Thursdays and Saturdays, listen to the very good live music.

LITTLE TOAD CREEK INN AND TAVERN

1122 Highway 35, Lake Roberts, 88061
575-536-9649, www.littletoadcreek.com
Taproom: At the Inn and Tavern and at Little Toad Creek Brewery and Distillery, 200
North Bullard Street, Silver City.

Some people might say that Little Toad Creek Inn and Tavern, one of New Mexico's newest craft breweries, is "in the middle of nowhere" or "off the beaten track." Certainly it's far from the nearest interstate—more than eighty miles and a two-hour drive from Interstate 25, along the very winding New Mexico Highway 152. But it would be fairer to say the brewpub, restaurant and lodge, located near the intersection of New Mexico Highways 15 and 35, is above and beyond, figuratively and literally. It is certainly beyond New Mexico's busy cities and crowded interstates, and at six thousand feet elevation, it's situated above more than two-thirds of the state's craft breweries. And it is above and beyond most areas in its natural beauty, abundant wildlife and amazing historical sites. Mountain lions, javelinas, black bears, white-nosed coati, Mexican gray wolves and countless species of birds, both familiar and rare, inhabit the wildernesses bordering the "Trail of the Mountain Spirits." The area was the home of the "Mimbres" culture, a society of now-gone Native Americans whose traditions are celebrated at the Mimbres Culture Heritage Site and the Gila Cliff Dwellings.

Teresa Dahl-Bredine and Dave Crosley, both natives of Silver City, had wanted to move into a more rural area when they discovered that the Breathe Inn, vacant for two years, was for sale. Located at edge of Sapillo Creek (*sapillo* means "little toad" in Spanish), it was quiet and peaceful but on a main tourist road and not too far away from Silver City.

"We realized that a restaurant, brewpub and inn were all necessary; each supported the other," Teresa noted. Given the kinds of tourists who would be traveling past the spot—outdoors enthusiasts, frequenters of art shops and students of traditional cultures—a restaurant (the only one in twenty miles) with an attached brewpub stood a good chance of succeeding. The scenic location would also entice people to become lodgers.

The bar; the restaurant; the nanobrewery; a very small distillery that produces rum, vodka and whiskey; and some of the guest rooms occupy the main building. More guest rooms are in the adjacent "Bunkhouse." Soon after Little Toad Creek Inn opened in the spring of 2013, it became a

Husband-and-wife team Dave Crosley and Teresa Dahl-Bredine are the owners of Little Toad Creek, a restaurant, lodge, nanobrewery and nanodistillery located near the Gila National Wilderness. *Courtesy the author.*

popular place for weddings, anniversaries and other group celebrations for people from Silver City and beyond.

Silver City, which had once been so conservative a beer-drinking town that a bar stocking the well-known Sierra Nevada Pale Ale was taking a considerable risk of not selling the product, had become more accepting of craft beer. "Having Western New Mexico University there certainly helped us, as many professors and students were familiar with craft beer. We felt many people would come out from town to try our brews," Crosley noted, adding that the restaurant also stocked Budweiser and other mainstream beers to please the recreational motorcyclists who often stopped for a drink and something to eat on weekend excursions.

Dahl-Bredine described the food at Little Toad Creek as "rustic gourmet." As they look out the picture windows of the bar and restaurant, enjoying the majestic scenery of the Gila wilderness, patrons can order such items as in-house smoked salmon, shrimp and queso, stuffed mushrooms, hazelnut crusted tilapia and apricot-chipotle chicken Alfredo. Weekend brunches, which are popular with people from Silver City, as well as with tourists, include blue corn pancakes, frittata and loco moco, which is described as a half-pound beef patty on rice, topped with gravy and two eggs.

And, of course, there is the beer, both brewed on site and industrially produced. Sam Costello, a Silver City home-brewer, has created three house beers. "We don't want beers that push the envelope at this time. We felt that we had to start gradually. And we don't want the beers to be too strong. The road our guests have to drive when they leave here is very winding. So we aim for consistently delicious beer," Crosley noted. Puppy Love Amber is a 5.4 percent ABV, medium-bodied, malty drink, designed as a gateway beer. As the nickname suggests, Crosley and Costello hope that this will be novice drinkers' first but not last craft beer love. Misty Mountain, Little Toad Creek's obligatory IPA, is 5.9 percent ABV. Thinking of the driving visitors, Crosley decided to make it much lower in alcoholic content than many other New Mexico versions of the style. It is a smooth-tasting, medium-bodied drink, with a pleasing balance of hop and malt flavors. Dave and Sam's Oatmeal Stout (6 percent ABV) is a blend of Irish and American styles, with chocolate notes.

MIMBRES VALLEY BREWING COMPANY

200 South Gold Avenue, Deming, 88030
575-544-2739, www.demingbrew.com
Taproom: At the brewery and at Las Cruces Taproom, 985 East University Avenue, Las Cruces

Like many aficionados of craft beer, Bryan Reedy had an "Aha!" moment that ended many years of drinking fizzy, pale yellow beers. When he was stationed at Kings Bay Naval Base in southern Georgia, one of his buddies who had traveled in Europe suggested that they go to a brewpub to "try some real beer." That was when Bryan discovered pale ales and stouts.

His military duties soon over, Reedy returned to his hometown of Deming, in southern New Mexico. "At first, I thought about opening a bar," he remembered. "But the cost of a full liquor license was in six figures. I attended the Craft Beer Conference in Boston in 2009, and that's when I decided to start a microbrewery. My father, Jim, became my partner."

Mimbres Valley Brewing Company and its brewpub are located at the main intersection of downtown Deming. *Courtesy the author.*

"I had no brewing experience, but I bought equipment anyway," Reedy continued. "I thought I could hire a brewer, but there weren't any available at the time. So I had to learn myself. Jeff Erway [La Cumbre], Rich Weber [Sierra Blanca] and Casey McFadden [Socorro Springs] really mentored me. It was a steep learning curve. One time the yeast blew up on me—now I always have an extra set of clothes. How I didn't get hurt, I don't know."

In 2010, Mimbres Valley Brewing opened at the corner of Spruce and Gold, downtown Deming's busiest intersection. It's the latest of a long list of business to occupy the building, which opened at the beginning of the twentieth century as Ray's Meat Market. The tin roof, wooden booths and mirror-backed bar give the brewpub a retro look. Tacked above the bar are several dozen dollar bills. One is the first the business earned; the others have been contributed by customers.

"Since we opened in 2010, we've offered thirty-five different beer styles, trying to see what worked. Our first beers were a lager, something

Dollar bills donated by customers line the wall behind Mimbres Valley Brewing's owner, Bryan Reedy. *Courtesy the author.*

that would be similar to what the local beer drinkers were used to, and an apricot wheat beer, which would be a little different but not threatening. Some people left when they discovered we didn't have Bud or Coors, but most stayed and tried what we had. We don't cater to hopheads; the locals like their beers to have balance. We lean toward English and German styles."

Mimbres Valley offers four year-round beers. Beer Goggles is a Vienna-style lager. The name is intended as a joke. "Beer goggles are standard safety equipment—something I soon learned," he said, laughing. "And people think that drinking beer is like wearing goggles; you see things differently." Pancho Villa Stout, named after the Mexican general who attacked southern New Mexico in 1916, is a sweet stout that uses Irish yeast. Silver Spike IPA is an English version of the style, offering a greater hop-malt balance than American West Coast versions. The name refers to the spike driven into the railway tracks at the edge of town in 1881, celebrating the completion of America's second transcontinental railroad. Liquid Nap is a Belgian tripel. At 9.2 percent ABV, it is Mimbres Valley's first "big" beer. The Trappist yeast gives it fruity notes.

Green chile beer is frequently available, particularly during the fall harvest season. "People think that Hatch is the chile capital of New Mexico," Bryan observed. "But here in Luna County, we grow and roast a lot more chiles." Its base beer is a helles lager, the malty notes of which offer a complement to the chile flavors. Perhaps the most unusual beer is Ugly Chick Ale. It was supposed to be a fairly standard IPA, but with New Zealand hops. "I was very sick the day we brewed, and I had an assistant doing most of the work. When it came time to pitch the yeast, he used a Belgian yeast by mistake."

In addition to beer, Reedy also makes mead and cider. The brewery has a small kitchen that prepares fried okra and fried pickles, along with sweet potato fries; chicken tenders; burgers, one of which is called "Hangover" and uses jalapeño bacon; grilled sandwiches; salads; and wings.

ROOSEVELT BREWING COMPANY & PUBLIC HOUSE

201 South Main Street, Portales, 88130
575-226-2729, www.rooseveltbrewing.com
Taproom: At the brewery.

"When we were renovating this place," remembered Justin Cole, owner of Roosevelt Brewing Company & Public House, "I used to sleep in the building. Main Street was empty after five o'clock. It was pretty lonely." By early 2013, that situation had changed. Main Street in downtown Portales was much busier in the evening. And one of the primary reasons was the brewpub that Cole and his friends had opened in 2012 in a 1920s building that had housed a J.C. Penney store and, most recently, a weight loss clinic.

Cole, who had been born and raised in nearby Clovis, had the idea for starting a brewpub while studying chemical engineering at New Mexico Technological University in Socorro. The city was home to Socorro Springs Brewpub. Justin, who had taken up home-brewing as a weekend hobby, worked in the kitchen there and familiarized himself with the operations of a brewpub. "I saw parallels between Socorro and Portales. Both were smaller towns that hosted universities." But Portales didn't have a brewpub.

The remodeling, more than $750,000 of it, became a process of historical discovery in a way. While shoring up the basement beams and posts so that they would support the first-floor brewing system, they uncovered a wall-sized poster advertising the 1939 move *Honolulu*, starring Eleanor Powell. The poster now adorns a large portion of one of the brewpub's walls. When they removed the first floor's lowered ceiling, they found the original molded tin tiles and, under several layers of floor coverings, the original hardwood. Both the tiles and the hardwood have been kept as part of the brewpub.

The building is long and narrow, fitting the configuration that it had long ago as a small-town department store. The walls are painted in what is called "Candy Apple Red," with large unplastered patches being a contrasting black. There are no television sets. "People come here to enjoy conversation, good food and good beer," Cole explained. Beyond the bar and seating area is the ten-barrel brewing system, and across from this is the kitchen, which is dominated by a wood-fired oven in which are prepared pizzas, the house breads and cupcakes (the only dessert). The oven is also used to roast the chiles used in the green chile beer. "It imparts a smoky note to the beer," Cole said.

Describing the house beers, Cole remarked, "Our goal is to brew our beers to style and to brew them well. We want them to be complex, but we don't want them to be too strong or too hoppy. I like English-style session beers, where you can enjoy the malt and yeast characteristics." The brewpub's first beers were an English-style pale ale, Portales Ale, with a 5.5 percent ABV, and Eleanor's Blonde, also a 5.5 percent ABV drink. The hop notes in each are understated; malty flavors take the forefront. The blonde ale is the bestseller. It is a gentle crossover beer, designed to lead people away from the American pale lagers that have dominated the area for decades.

Other beers include Wind Blown Berliner Weisse (3.5 percent ABV), Happy Heifer Hefeweizen (4.9 percent ABV), Dirt Town Brown (an English-style 4.0 percent session beer), Clovis Point IPA (a West Coast–style IPA) and green chile beer (which uses a kolsch as its base). The dark side of the spectrum is represented by Big Stick Stout and Cole Espresso Porter.

It didn't take long for Roosevelt Brewing Company & Public House to catch on with the beer-drinking public of Roosevelt County. "In the first few weeks, we kept running out of our beer, especially the blonde, people were so enthusiastic." Pretty soon Main Street wasn't deserted in the evenings.

THE WELLHEAD RESTAURANT AND BREWPUB

332 West Main Street, Artesia, 88210
575-746-0640, www.thewellhead.com
Taproom: At the brewery.

As owner Frank Yates remembered it, the idea for The Wellhead was born in the later 1990s in the garage of his home-brewing brother, Mike Stegall. He jokingly said that the two may have enjoyed a little too much beer at the time. Frank, a prominent citizen in the southeastern New Mexico city and a major player in the area's petroleum industry, saw a brewpub not only as a place where locals could quench their thirst but also as a contribution to Artesia MainStreet, an organization overseeing the project to renovate city-center buildings in order to bring businesses and citizens back downtown.

He chose as the location for his brewpub a building that was kitty-corner to the Yates Petroleum headquarters. Erected in 1905, it had originally been the home of the Madison Hotel and Sample Room. In April 2000, after two years of restoration and renovation, The Wellhead Restaurant and Brewpub opened. It was decorated as a celebration of the oil industry that had come to Artesia in the 1920s. A large tiled mosaic depicted the Illinois #3 well, the gusher that transformed the Eddy County economy from agricultural to petroleum based. Pictures and small signs relate to the oil industry, lampshades and the fountain on the summer patio resemble oil derricks and the names of several of the beers refer to the area's main business: Wellhead Pale Ale, Roughneck Red, Crude Oil Stout and Wildcat IPA. There's even a humorous (and nonexistent) item on the menu that refers to an oilman's worst fear. "Back by Very Unpopular Demand," the description reads, "Dry Hole Special—Empty Bowl with a Spoon." The price is listed at $2,324,912.17.

There are also real items of the menu, most of them typical of southwestern pub fare: wings, fried pub peppers, potato skins, green chile stew, the Big Rig Burger, catfish, steaks, chicken and salmon. The Tuesday night special is meatloaf with mashed potatoes and gravy. "It is very popular. Some people come in every week for it," said The Wellhead's general manager Emily Bills.

Since its opening, The Wellhead has employed four brewers. Yates's brother, Mike, was the first, working until 2003; he left for a job that would make it easier to put his children through college. Diane Riley and Bill Geldreich followed. Since 2011, Tom Crumrine, whose father holds the

The Wellhead is one of the many renovated buildings in Artesia's revitalized downtown. *Courtesy the author.*

number-two membership in The Wellhead's mug club—Frank Yates holds number one—has been the brewer.

A local boy, Tom remembered his father taking him on business trips, which often included having meals in brewpubs. "I was certainly aware of craft beer," he explained. "But it wasn't until I went to Germany as an exchange student that I discovered how good beer could be. I loved the German lagers—they were so crisp, clean and clear." By high school, he had become a home-brewer and recalled hanging around The Wellhead, watching brewer Diane Riley at work and asking her frequent questions.

When he came to Albuquerque to study accounting at the University of New Mexico, Tom enjoyed spending time, perhaps not legally, at two of the city's growing number of brewpubs and taprooms. "I became a regular when Marble opened in 2008, and later I got a job as the first manager at the Il Vicino Canteen." At Il Vicino, he watched Brady McKeown and his "Brew Crew" at work and even helped during the mashing and boiling phases of brewing. "I wasn't twenty-one, and so I wasn't allowed to pitch yeast or do any of the work relating to the fermenting and conditioning of

Brewer Tom Crumrine stands in front of a miniature oil derrick, one of the brewpub's many decorations that celebrate the importance of the petroleum industry in southeast New Mexico. *Courtesy the author.*

the beer." Shortly after he turned twenty-one, The Wellhead advertised for a new brewer, and with McKeown's strong encouragement, he applied, was accepted and returned to his hometown.

The beer list he inherited was basically what had been introduced when The Wellhead opened in 2000. Given the fact that many of the customers have been people familiar with the products of the big industrial brewers, it's not surprising that the majority of the beers are lower in alcohol and IBUs than is the case with most craft beers. Four of the regular offerings are under 5.0 percent ABV; the most potent of the regulars is Wild Cat IPA, a whopping 7.5 percent ABV and 75 IBUs. The bestseller is Cisco Canyon Blonde. Named after a nearby area that is rich in oil-producing shale, it is 4.8 percent ABV and has very little hop presence.

Crumrine described the blonde as light and crisp. "It's like a kolsch, but I use English malts to make it maltier." Wellhead Pale is designed to be a middle-of-the-line version of the style, medium bodied and not very bitter (only 25 IBUs). His version of Roughneck Red is, he remarked, inspired by New Belgium's Fat Tire. "It has some malty sweetness." Wildcat IPA is "my hop bomb. It's dry and bitter. I made it for IPA lovers and didn't dull it down." One of his more unusual beers is made with prickly pears. Pinkish, smooth tasting and both dry and sweet, it uses a Belgian white ale as its base and adds a prickly pear puree.

The Wellhead's beers are created with an awareness of both the physical and social landscape of Eddy County. "It gets very hot here," Crumrine explained, "so we want something dry, crisp and refreshing. We don't want to brew something that is too full-bodied. We want our beers to be tasty and accessible. They certainly have lower alcohol and hop rates than you'd find in Albuquerque. But some of the people around here still think that they're too strong!"

EPILOGUE

THE EXPANDING
"FRONTIER OF BEER"

In the early spring of 2012, when I began planning my excursions to the "Frontier of Beer," twenty-three breweries operated in New Mexico. At the end of September 2013, by the time I had finished my visits, samplings, interviews, research and writing, eleven new breweries had begun operation. One of the twenty-three had gone out of business. The "Frontier of Beer" had certainly expanded.

And there was no sign that the expansion was ending or even slowing down. Santa Fe Brewing, La Cumbre, Bosque and Blue Corn announced that they would be increasing their production facilities. Tractor moved from Los Lunas to a large new facility in Albuquerque, and Little Toad Creek opened a taproom in Silver City, while Bosque announced that it would open a taproom in Albuquerque's Nob Hill area. Bosque also announced that John Bullard, who won two Great American Beer Festival medals for Blue Corn Café and Brewery in 2013, would become its head brewer in the early spring of 2014.

Two breweries opened late in the fall of 2013, three more were scheduled to open in the early part of 2014 and construction on two more was scheduled to begin later in 2014. The two new breweries were Desert Water Brewing of Artesia and Branding Iron Brewery in Silver City. Desert Water, located just north of Artesia at 1 East Cottonwood Road, is a division of Cottonwood Wine and Brewing, run by Michael Mahan. Available in the taproom are an amber ale, a pilsner, an Irish red, a wheat beer and a stout, along with snacks. Branding Iron is part of Q's Southern Bistro located at

101 West College Avenue in Silver City. Brewers Anthony Panchero and Bob Brockhausen offer a red, an amber, an IPA and a Mexican lager. Plans are to open a taproom in Las Cruces.

During the early months of 2014, the Albuquerque brew scene will experience a West Coast "invasion" of sorts. Stumbling Steer Brewery will open on the city's west side (3700 Ellison Road NW). Two of the partners of this gastropub, General Manager Sonny Jensen and award-winning brewer Kirk Roberts, served in similar positions at the Beer Company in San Diego. Pints Brewing located in Portland, Oregon's Old Town will run an as-yet-unnamed brewpub in the Sawmill District north of Albuquerque's Old Town (1761 Bellamah Avenue NW). Alan Taylor, head brewer for the Portland operation, promised that the beer list will offer "something malty, something hoppy, and something yeasty." In addition, B2B Bistronomy, a gourmet hamburger restaurant located at 3118 Central Avenue SE in Albuquerque's Nob Hill, planned to install a small brewing system to create what owner Sham Naik called "gourmet beers" to complement the thirty-two taps of New Mexico beers already offered.

Later in 2014, Jim Schull plans to open Hops, a brewpub in Albuquerque's Nob Hill (3507 Central Avenue NE), bringing to seven the number of brewpubs and taprooms in the area just east of the University of New Mexico. Joel and Deanna Green plan to have Roadrunner Ale House up and running late in the fall of 2014. It will be located across the street from New Mexico State University in Las Cruces (901 East University Avenue, Suite 945A). The young couple, who celebrated their graduation from New Mexico State by visiting seventy-five craft breweries and brewpubs in the western states and then went on to become certified beer judges, will offer locally sourced food and a range of ales from light to dark. It has been unofficially reported that Socorro Springs Restaurant and Brewhouse may be sold and that new owners would consider reinstalling a brew house.

Why has there been such a rapid expansion, and why does there appear to be no indication that it will abate in the near future?

Christopher Goblet, director of the New Mexico Brewers Guild, attributed the growth to the fact that "the market is not saturated. In fact, it's barely tapped." He went on to note that many brewers who are currently operating are having to expand their brew houses so that they can keep up with demand. Goblet also said that the state government has created an environment that is hospitable to craft brewers. Brewers in the state are permitted to sell beer to other brewers without having to use third-party distribution companies. Each brewery can operate three taprooms, which provide excellent places to showcase their beers, particularly new and often unusual styles. And beginning in 2014, breweries will be able to make up to ten thousand barrels per year, up from five thousand, at the very low taxation rate of eight cents per gallon. Above ten thousand barrels, the rate is twenty-eight cents per gallon and forty cents above fifteen thousand.

Goblet also noted that the beer-drinking public in New Mexico has become used to beers that are of very high quality. The number of people who drink beers produced in the state has grown steadily because, quite simply, the beer is very good. The fact that New Mexican brewers regularly return from the annual Great American Beer Festival with medals is a confirmation that there is an abundance of very talented and imaginative makers of beer in the Land of Enchantment. "There's an amazing level of cooperation and competition amongst them," Goblet said. "They do help each other, and when someone produces an exceptional beer, it raises the bar for everyone else."

"You can make the best beer in the world," an old brewer's saying goes, "but if nobody buys it, it doesn't mater." New Mexico brewers are fortunate to have a growing and increasingly more knowledgeable coterie of supporters. They read articles about beer in local daily newspapers and free newspapers. They attend the expanding number of beer festivals held around the state throughout the year. And perhaps most importantly, they visit the taprooms found at nearly all of New Mexico's breweries. There they have the chance to enjoy fresh beer created only a few yards away; they can meet the men and women who make the beer, learning some "secrets" about the brew they are sipping. The beer aficionados talk to one another, comparing beers they have tasted. They are particularly harsh in their judgments of bad beer. The New Mexico breweries that have failed in recent years have done so in part because customers have found their beers inconsistent from one batch to the next, bland (which is worse) or downright bad.

Summing up the state of New Mexico beer in the fall of 2013, Goblet enthusiastically stated, "We've just seen the beginning of what New Mexico has to offer. It's going to get bigger and better."

I'll drink to that!

BEER STYLES AND NEW MEXICO EXAMPLES

The following guide to beer styles is divided into three sections: lagers, ales and specialty beers. Following each description are some New Mexican examples. In putting together the style descriptions, I have drawn on Randy Mosher's *Tasting Beer: An Insider's Guide to the World's Greatest Drink* (North Adams, MA: Storey Publishing, 2009), Garrett Oliver's *The Brewmaster's Table* (New York: HarperCollins, 2003) and Dan Rabin and Carl Forget's *The Dictionary of Beer and Brewing* (Boulder, CO: Brewers Publications, 2008). In each issue of *All About Beer* magazine, there is an article on a specific beer style.

LAGERS

Lagers use bottom-fermenting yeast, are generally more highly carbonated and are lighter-bodied than most ales. With the development of refrigeration in the later part of the nineteenth century, lagers, which must be brewed and stored at lower temperatures, have become very popular in the United States, where brewers from Germany, the birthplace of most lagers, created versions of the beers of their homeland and established very large breweries and extensive distribution networks. Varieties of North American pale lagers are the most widely consumed beers in the world.

bock: A German-style beer with much fuller body and more robust flavors than other lagers. Lightly hopped, it is dark in color—from copper to a deep brown—and medium- to full-bodied. *Blue Corn JB's Log Splitter Helles Bock, Chama River Winter Lager, High Desert Dark Bock, High Desert Pale Bock, La Cumbre Cabra Fuerte Bock, La Cumbre Weizenbock, Tractor BarnStorm Heller Bock.*

Bohemian (Czech) pilsner: A light-bodied and clear, light straw to golden-colored beer, with a crispness imparted by the hops. It was originally brewed in Pilsen, where the soft water enhanced the crisp cleanness of the beer. *Chama River Czech Saaz Pilsner, De La Vega's Gelbe Schnee Bohemian Pilsner, High Desert Bohemian Pilsner, La Cumbre South Peak Pilsner, New Mexico Pilsner.*

California common beer: Also called "steam beer" because of the hissing sound when a keg is tapped, this style was developed in California in the nineteenth century. This amber beer is medium-bodied and is fairly highly hopped. Anchor Steam Brewing Company of California has copyrighted the name "steam beer." *Broken Bottle Steamy Lawyer; High Desert Steam Beer; La Cumbre Ooh Baby, I'm Common; New Mexico Cerveza de Vapor; Second Street Rod's Steam Bitter; Sierra Blanca Rio Grande Outlaw Lager; Turtle Mountain Mr. Hoover's Steam.*

doppelbock: Stronger in alcoholic content and more full-bodied and darker colored than bock, this style often has chocolate and coffee tastes. *Blue Heron Doppel Bock.*

Dortmunder Export: Pale gold in color, with a medium hop bitterness and a crisp finish. The malts contribute biscuit flavors to this medium-bodied beer. *La Cumbre No, You're a Dort!; Marble Thunder from Dortmunder.*

dunkel: Full-bodied and light to dark brown in color, this is a full-bodied lager with rich malty flavors. *La Cumbre Munchener Dunkel.*

German pilsner: A light- to medium-bodied, straw to gold lager that has spicy hop notes and a slight malt sweetness. It is fuller in body and maltier than Czech pilsners. *Blue Corn Atomic Blonde Lager, Blue Heron Oro de Rio Grande Pilsner, De La Vega's D's German Pilsner, Il Vicino Pigtail Pilsner, Marble Pilsner, Sandia Chile Grill Double Pilsner, Sandia Chile Grill Gold Rush Pilsner, Santa Fe Freestyle Pilsner, Sierra Blanca Rio Grande Desert Pils, Tractor #15 (aka Minneapolis/ Moline), Turtle Mountain Vanilla Cocoa Dark Lager (Imperial).*

helles: From the German word meaning "bright," this medium-bodied beer balances malt and hop flavors. Light straw to golden in color, it often features toasty malt flavors. *Chama River Class VI Golden Lager, La Cumbre Where in the Helles Beer?*

maibock: A golden-colored bock beer available in the later spring (May). It is distinguished by its sweet malty notes and relatively light body. *Blue Heron XXX Maibock, Tractor Maibock.*

marzen: Full-bodied, very malty, copper-colored beer with a crisp hop bitterness. *Il Vicino Marzen.*

Mexican lager: See Vienna lager.

North American lager: Pale in color, very light in body and highly carbonated, with minimal hop and malt flavors. *De La Vega's D's Light American Lager, La Cumbre BEER, Marble Bier.*

Oktoberfest: A medium-bodied autumn beer that has smooth caramel malt flavors that are balanced with a hop bitterness. *Blue Corn Oktoberfest, High Desert Oktoberfest, Santa Fe Oktoberfest, Tractor Tractoberfest.*

rauchbier: From the German *rauch* for "smoke," a dark-colored lager using malt roasted over open fires to impart a smoky flavor. *Comanche Creek Old Smoky, La Cumbre Hot Shorts Rauch.*

schwarzbier: From the German word *schwarz* for "black," a very dark-colored light- to medium-bodied beer. The roasted barley malts impart chocolaty flavors that are balanced with a low to medium hop bitterness. *Chama River Liquid Schwarz, Eske's Black Cat, Marble Dark Secret, Mimbres Valley Black Lager, Second Street Schwarzbier.*

Vienna lager: Medium-bodied and reddish-brown to copper, this lager has a malty sweetness balanced with a clean and crisp but not too strong hop bitterness. Mexican lagers are a variation of the Vienna lager style. *Blue Corn Vienna Lager, High Desert Amber Lager, Il Vicino Dark American Lager, Las Cazuela's Acapulco Gold, Mimbres Valley Beer Goggles Lager, Second Street Tres Equis Lager, Three Rivers Oscura Vienna.*

ALES

Using top-fermenting yeast, ales do not require the cooler temperatures for fermenting and conditioning that lagers do, and the brewing cycles are much shorter. Generally speaking, ales are fuller-bodied, darker in color and richer and more robust in flavor. When the craft brewing movement began in the late 1970s and early 1980s, most microbrewers produced ales, offering beers that were different in taste from those of the megabrewers.

alt bier: From the German word *alt* meaning "old" (traditional), this copper to brown ale has toasted malty flavors balanced by hop notes that help to create a clean, crisp finish. *Comanche Creek Homestead Amber, Kellys Alt Bier, Second Street Alternator Dubbel Alt, Second Street German Alt Bier.*

amber ale: This copper to light-brown beer has been called a "darker fuller-bodied pale ale." It maintains a balance between caramel malt notes and citrusy hop flavors. *Abbey Brewing Monks Ale (Belgian style), Blue Corn Atalaya Amber, Blue Heron Amber's Folly Amber, Bosque Brewer's Boot Amber, Chama River Amber, De La Vega's Aggie Amber, Duel Bad Amber (Belgian style), High Desert Amber, Il Vicino Dougie Style Amber, Kellys Amber, La Cumbre Pyramid Rock Amber, Marble Amber, Nexus Amber, Sandia Chile Grill Smooth Move Amber, Sierra Blanca Alien Amber, Three Rivers Arroyo Amber, Turtle Mountain Gluten-Free Amber.*

American blonde/golden ale: Lightly to moderately hopped, this straw to golden-blonde beverage is a light-bodied and crisp beer that is often offered as a "crossover" beer to newcomers to craft beer. *Blue Corn Lakeside Summer Ale, Blue Heron Embudo Gold Golden, Bosque Kindling Ale, Comanche Creek Gold Rush Golden, Il Vicino Pig Tail Blonde, Kellys Golden, Roosevelt Eleanor's Blonde, Taos Ale House La Rubia Ale, The Wellhead Cisco Canyon Blonde.*

American dark ale (aka Cascadian dark ale/black IPA): A recently developed American style, this dark-brown to black-colored beer combines roasty malt flavors with a strong hop presence. *Broken Bottle The Incident Black IPA, Chama River Shadow Boxer Black IPA, High Desert Black IPA, Il Vicino Cascadian Dark, Santa Fe Black IPA, Tractor Black IPA, Turtle Mountain Ironman Black IPA, The Wellhead Smoking Black IPA.*

American strong ale: Ales noted for their higher alcoholic content, usually above 7 percent alcohol by volume: *Back Alley American Strong, Chama River Dr. HopGood, Il Vicino Fruitcake Strong Ale.*

American wheat ale: An American version of *hefeweizen* that is frequently filtered. *Chama River American Wheat, De La Vega's D's Wheat, High Desert Wheat, Sierra Blanca Alien Wheat, Three Rivers Bare Naked Aggie Wheat, Turtle Mountain American Wheat.*

barley wine: High in alcoholic content (usually over 10 percent alcohol by volume), this has been called a "sipping beer." It is full-bodied and dark brown in color and has complex malt flavors that include caramel, toasty and fruity notes. *Broken Bottle Cracked Cork Barley Wine, Chama River High Five Anniversary Ale, Eske's Bert & Ernie Barley Wine, High Desert Barleywine, Marble Barleywine, Mimbres Valley Barley Wine, New Mexico Tooth Puller, Santa Fe Chicken Killer Barley Wine, Second Street Barley Wine-Style Ale, Tractor Barleywine, The Wellhead Barley Wine.*

Belgian blonde/golden ale: Light- to medium-bodied, gold to deep amber in color, this ale has a malty sweetness, spicy notes and moderate hoppiness. *Duel Titian Strong Belgium Style Golden Ale.*

Belgian dark ale: Ranging in color from amber to garnet, this medium-bodied beer balances dry and spicy notes with rich, malty sweetness. *Duel Dark Ryder Dark Ale.*

Belgian India pale ale: See India pale ale.

Belgian strong ale: Stronger in flavor and alcoholic content and fuller in body than Belgian dark. *Blue Corn Golden Strong Ale, Marble Abbey Darkness.*

bitter: The beer that is most often associated with an evening at English pubs, it has a balance between malt sweetness and hop bitterness, with earthy, nutty and grainy flavors. Light-bodied and gold to copper in color, it is low in carbonation and in alcoholic content (usually under 5 percent alcohol by volume). *Eske's Artist Ale, Eske's Special Bitter, Kellys Black Bitter.*

brown ale: Brown ale is noted for its rich malt flavors, including nutty, toffee and chocolate notes. This medium-bodied beer is generally sweet, although moderate hopping prevents the sweetness from becoming overwhelming. *Blue Corn End of the Trail Brown, Blue Heron Adobe Brown, Bosque Mellow Brit, Chama River Beast of Bourbon Brown, Chama River Rio Lodo, De La Vega's Vanilla Oak Brown, Eske's Brown-Eyed, Il Vicino Slow Down Brown, Kellys Brown, La Cumbre Hell Froze Over Brown, Marble Belgo Brown, Nexus Brown, Roosevelt Dirt Town Brown, Santa Fe Nut Brown, Second Street Brown, Sierra Blanca Nut Brown, Taos Mesa Fall Down Brown, Three Rivers LeRoy Brown Imperial Brown, Turtle Mountain Grandma's Brown.*

cream ale: Straw to pale gold in color, this light-bodied ale is high in carbonation but low in hop bitterness and has a malty sweetness. *Nexus Cream, Nexus Imperial Cream.*

dark mild: A popular session beer that is light- to medium-bodied and gold to dark brown in color. Fairly low in alcohol (usually under 5 percent alcohol by volume) and in carbonation, it has almost no hop flavors. Sweet chocolate and caramel malt flavors dominate. *Second Street British Mild.*

dubbel: A Belgian ale noted for its rich, malty flavors and spicy notes. Dark amber to brown, it is lightly hopped. Generally sweet to the taste, with a light to moderate bitterness, it has a dry finish. *Abbey Brewing Monks' Dubbel, De La Vega's Abbey Ale, Kellys Belgian Dubbel, La Cumbre Dubbel Entendre, Santa Fe Visalay Belgian, Second Street Dubbel.*

dunkelweizen: A wheat beer that uses dark malts and is sweeter than hefeweizen. *Kellys Dunkelweizen, Taos Ale House Dunkelweizen.*

extra special bitter (ESB): A popular English-style beer, it is more full-bodied and higher in alcoholic content than a bitter. Although it has more bitterness than a bitter, rich, malty flavors dominate. Dark gold to copper in color, it is low in carbonation. *High Desert Extra Special Bitter, Il Vicino ESB, Las Cazuela's ESB, Kellys ESB, Second Street Rod's Best Bitter, Taos Mesa Notorious ESB.*

Flanders *oud bruin*: This centuries-old Belgian style is light to medium in body and deep copper to brown in color. It is both sweet and spicy. The use of burnt sugar contributes to the sweetness, while the yeasts and such additives as pepper provide spicy notes. *Marble Oude Brune.*

hefeweizen: From the German words for "yeast" and "wheat," this pale- to amber-colored ale has been called "liquid bread." Generally close to 50 percent of the malt used is wheat. Highly carbonated, it has virtually no hop character, but it does have banana and clove notes. Because it is unfiltered, it has a hazy appearance. *Bosque Engaano Hefeweizen, Broken Bottle David Hasselheffe, Eske's Hula Hoop Hefeweizen, High Desert Hefeweizen, Kellys Weizen, La Cumbre A Slice of Hefen, Las Cazuela's Hefeweizen, Roosevelt Happy Heifer, Sandia Chile Grill Barb's Barrel Hefeweizen, Santa Fe Hefeweizen.*

India pale ale (IPA): This pale gold to amber ale is more heavily hopped than pale ales. In English IPAs, the hop influence is moderated somewhat by the malts, which add bready, caramel notes. American IPAs are much more aggressively hopped, increasing the bitterness and also adding citrusy and floral tastes. Double or Imperial IPAs are fuller-bodied, intensely hoppy and higher in alcoholic content (from 7 to 10 percent alcohol by volume). Belgian IPAs are noted for their bitterness, dryness and high alcoholic content. *Blue Corn Head Honcho Imperial IPA, Blue Corn Road Runner IPA, Blue Heron Cascabel IPA, Bosque Ember IPA, Bosque Wheat IPA, Broken Bottle Year Two IPA, Chama River Captain's Chair IPA, Chama River Dangerous Intensions Imperial IPA, Chama River Hop Slap Imperial IPA, Chama River Jackalope IPA, Comanche Creek Touch-Me-Not IPA, De La Vega's Double IPA, Duel Fiction Belgian IPA, High Desert IPA, Il Vicino Exodus IPA, Il Vicino Wet Mountain IPA, Kellys India Pale Ale, La Cumbre Elevated IPA, La Cumbre Project Dank: Operation Pharaoh's Return, Las Cazuela's Chupacabra IPA, Las Cazuela's Papacabra Double IPA, Marble Double India Pale Ale, Marble India Pale Ale, Mimbres Valley Silver Spike IPA, Mimbres Valley Ugly Chick Belgian IPA, New Mexico Starvation Peak Indian Pale Ale, Nexus IPA, Sandia Chile Grill Rattlesnake India Pale Ale, Santa Fe Happy Camper IPA, Second Street IPA, Sierra Blanca Rio Grande India Pale Ale, Taos Ale House Mogul Imperial IPA, Taos Ale House Stone Lake IPA, Taos Mesa Hopper IPA, Three Rivers IPA, Tractor Farmer's Almanac India Pale Ale, Turtle Mountain Hoptimus Pride Double IPA, Turtle Mountain Hybrid IPA, Turtle Mountain Wild Bill Hiccup's Oatmeal IPA, The Wellhead Wildcat IPA.*

Irish stout: See stout.

kolsch: Originally brewed in Koln, Germany, this beer has been jokingly referred to as "the ale that wishes it were a lager" because of its light body, pale color and higher carbonation. It balances gentle hop and malt flavors and has a crisp mouth feel and a dry finish. *Chama River Cold Crush Kolsch, Comanche Creek Kolsch, High Desert Kolsch, La Cumbre Miles from Cologne Kolsche, Second Street Kolsch, Taos Mesa Kolsch 45, Three Rivers Kolsch.*

kristalweizen: A clear, filtered, straw to light amber version of hefeweizen. *Sandia Chile Grill Kristalweizen.*

lambic: This four-hundred-year-old Belgian-style ale is unusual in that its fermentation process is natural or spontaneous, using wild yeast that is floating in the air. It has been described as fruity, earthy, sour or tart, as well as very dry. Gold to amber in color, it is light-bodied and low in carbonation. Unmalted wheat is used in the brewing process. Sometimes brewers will blend old (aged) lambic with young lambic to create a beer called gueuze, a dry, fruity, effervescent beer. In fruit lambics, whole fruits are added after the start of fermentation, and the resulting mixture is aged in oak or chestnut barrels—*kriek* uses cherries, *framboise* raspberries, *peche* peaches and *cassis* black currants. *Santa Fe Kriek.*

oatmeal stout: See stout.

pale ale: This gold to amber ale, which was much paler than the popular brown ales and porters of the late eighteenth century, balances nutty, caramel malt notes with a noticeable hop bitterness. English-style pale ale is earthier in flavor as contrasted to West Coast–style American pale ale, which has fuller hop bitterness, flavor and aroma. Both are crisp and have a dry finish. Belgian pale ale is less bitter than the other two, is lighter-bodied and has some malty sweetness. *Back Alley Pale Ale, Blue Corn Czech Your English, Blue Heron Lava Rock Pale Ale, Chama River Centennial Pale Ale, Chama River Copper John Pale Ale, Comanche Creek Dead Man Pale Ale, Duel Non-Fiction Belgian Pale Ale, Eske's Mesa Pale Ale, High Desert Pale Ale, Il Vicino Crystal Pale Ale, Kellys Belgian Pale Ale, Kellys British Pale Ale, Marble Chinook Pale Ale, Marble Rye Pale Ale, Roosevelt Portales Ale, Santa Fe Pale Ale, Second Street Ahtanum Pale Ale, Second Street Pajarito Pale Ale, Sierra Blanca Pale Ale, Taos Ale House Southwest Pale Ale, Taos Mesa Lunch Pale Ale, Three Rivers Animas Pale Ale, Three Rivers Smash EPA, Tractor Sod Buster Pale Ale, Turtle Mountain Hop Duster Pale Ale, Turtle Mountain Triple Play Pale Ale, The Wellhead Pale Ale.*

porter: Named after the late eighteenth-century London workers for whom it was originally brewed, this brown to black-colored and full-bodied ale uses several malts to create a complex variety of flavors. Relatively low in alcohol, it is moderately bitter. *Blue Corn Decadent Porter, Blue Heron Penasco Porter, Bosque Old Bosky Porter, Broken Bottle Glugg Porter, Chama River Porter for Pyros, Chama River 3 Dog Night Baltic Porter, Duel Grunewald Belgian Style Imperial*

Porter, *Eske's Oat Cole Porter, High Desert Porter, Kellys Robust Porter, Las Cazuela's Robusto Porter, Marble Imperial Porter, Mimbres Valley Brown Porter, Mimbres Valley Nacio Herb Brown Porter, New Mexico Pantyshot Porter, Roosevelt Cole Espresso Porter, Sandia Chile Grill Smoked Porter, Santa Fe State Pen Porter, Second Street Pecos Porter, Second Street 3 Cs Porter, Taos Ale House The Simple Porter, Three Rivers Baltic Porter, Turtle Mountain Arsenal Porter, The Wellhead Roustabout Porter.*

red ale: A light to highly hopped, medium-bodied, amber- or copper-colored beer, with toasted malt notes and a caramel sweetness. *Back Alley Red, Blue Corn Columbus Red, Blue Heron Tarantula Trek Red, Bosque Far Darrig Red, Broken Bottle AFD Red, Chama River Red, Duel Ensor Red, High Desert Irish Red, Il Vicino Irish Red, Kellys Red, La Cumbre Irish Red, Las Cazuela's Panama Red, Marble Imperial Red, Marble Red, New Mexico Ojo Rojo, Nexus Red, Sandia Chile Grill Sun Ranger Irish Red, Santa Fe Irish Red, Tractor Farmer's Tan Red, Tractor Tupac Cali Red, The Wellhead Roughneck Red.*

roggen: This German ale uses malted rye and is both spicy and sour, with a noticeable hop finish. *Back Alley Rye Wit, Back Alley White Ryeno, Chama River Whispering Rye, High Desert Rye Beer, Marble Roggenbier, Turtle Mountain Red Rye.*

saison/farmhouse ale: Designed as a beer with which farmworkers could quench their thirst during hot summer days in the fields, this Belgian-style ale is gold to amber in color, light- to medium-bodied and highly carbonated. It is spicy (white pepper is often used), moderately bitter, fruity and sour or tart. *Bosque Saison Rouge, Il Vicino Saison d'Guil, Marble Daisie Mae Saison, Santa Fe Saison 88, Taos Ale House Saison.*

Scotch ale/wee heavy: This strong, dark, creamy, full-bodied ale is mahogany in color. It has caramel flavors and sometimes, because of the malts used, smoky notes. *Bosque Scotia Scotch Ale, High Desert Scotch Ale, Tractor Oxbow Scotch Ale.*

Scottish ale: Designated as "light," "heavy" or "export" depending on the alcoholic content, this ale is not as strong as Scotch ale. Malt flavors dominate over hops. *Blue Heron La Llorona Scottish, Duel Manikin Scottish, Eske's Scottish, High Desert Scottish, Kellys Scottish, Nexus Scottish, Three Rivers Scottish.*

stout: Dark brown to opaque black, it is noted for the roasted flavors imparted by the malted and unmalted barley. English stout is a somewhat sweet ale with caramel and chocolate flavors that are balanced by the hop bitterness. Irish stout is drier than English versions and often has coffee and chocolate flavors. Designed to be a session beer, it is slightly lighter in body than English versions. Oatmeal stout, in which unmalted oatmeal is added in the brewing process, is very smooth in texture. Russian (Imperial Stout) has an alcoholic content above 10 percent ABV. It is not only more bitter than other stouts, it also has much fuller malt flavors. *Back Alley Imperial Russian Stout, Blue Corn Gold Medal Oatmeal Stout, Blue Heron Prieta Real Imperial Stout, Bosque Oatmeal Stout, Broken Bottle Mulligan Stout, Chama River Extra Stout, Chama River Sleeping Dog Stout, Duel Goya Imperial Stout, Eske's 10,000 Foot Stout, High Desert Stout, Il Vicino Dark and Lusty Stout, Il Vicino St. Bob's Bourbon Barrel Imperial Stout, Kellys Imperial Stout, Kellys Oatmeal Stout, La Cumbre Malpais Stout, Marble Imperial Stout, Marble Oatmeal Stout, Mimbres Valley Pancho Villa Stout, New Mexico Road House Oatmeal Stout, Nexus Stout, Sandia Chile Grill Rio Negro Nitro Milk Stout, Sandia Chile Grill Smoked Milk Stout, Santa Fe Java Stout, Second Street Cream Stout, Second Street Imperial Stout, Second Street Oatmeal Stout, Sierra Blanca Alien Imperial Stout, Taos Mesa Superstitious Stout, Three Rivers Rasputin's Imperial Stout, Three Rivers Thode's Fat Dog Stout, Tractor Double Plowed Oatmeal Stout, Tractor Mustachio Milk Stout, Turtle Mountain Cosmic Imperial Stout, Turtle Mountain Maduro Stout, The Wellhead Crude Oil Stout.*

tripel: Although lighter in body than dubbel, this Belgian ale is stronger in alcoholic content (7 to 10 percent alcohol by volume). Bright yellow to gold, it has spicy and fruity notes and a sweetness that is balanced by a moderate hop bitterness. *Abbey Brewing Monks' Tripel, Broken Bottle End of Day`s Tripel, Marble Tripel, Mimbres Valley Liquid Nap, Taos Ale House Hat Trick Belgian Tripel.*

witbier: From the Belgian word for "white," this unfiltered wheat beer is pale and cloudy in appearance. Highly carbonated and crisp, it is low- to medium-bodied and is often flavored with coriander and orange peel. *Abbey Brewing Monks' Wit, Chama River Imperial White, Duel Sour Belgian Wit, Il Vicino M 28, Marble Double White, Mimbres Valley Belgian Wit, Nexus White Ale, Tractor A Witty Belgian Ale, The Wellhead Indian Basin Wheat.*

SPECIALTY BEERS

In addition to creating a great variety of styles through their different uses of the four basic ingredients of beer (malts, hops, yeast and water), brewers often use such additives as fruits, vegetables, herbs, spices, honey, chocolate and coffee to introduce nuances of flavor. (In the following list, where the name of a beer does not indicate what additive is used, the additive is named in parentheses.)

chocolate and coffee beers: Note that while some malts can impart coffee and chocolate notes to a beer, only those beers that use coffee and chocolate are included in this list. *Blue Corn Chocolate Porter, Il Vicino Panama Joe's, Mimbres Valley Chocolate Pinon Coffee Stout.*

fruit beers: Note that Belgian fruit lambics are not included in this list. *Blue Heron Los Duraznos Peach Ale, Broken Bottle June Bug Summer Ale (lemon zest and paradise seed), Broken Bottle Tom Selleck Ale (cranberry), Chama River Apricot Wheat (aka Hopricot Wheat), Eske's President's Cherry Delite, High Desert Peach Wheat Ale, Il Vicino Milk Chocolate Cherry Stout, Kellys Apricot, Marble Cuvee d'Abricot, Marble Framboise, Three Rivers Orchard Street Raspberry Wheat Ale, Three Rivers Peachy Kean Wheat Ale, The Wellhead Prickly Pear.*

herb and spice beers: *Broken Bottle Anomole Stout (red chile and cinnamon), Broken Bottle Rosemary's Baby (rosemary), Broken Bottle Xico Sauve (fennel and caraway seed), Chama River Ginger Bread Beer, De La Vega's D's Green Chile Ale, Eske's Taos Green Chile Beer, Mimbres Valley Green Chile Lager, Sierra Blanca Rio Grande Pancho Verde Chili-Cerveza, Tractor Turkey Drool Christmas Ale.*

honey beers: *Blue Corn 40K Honey Wheat, Chama River Broken Spoke Honey Wheat, Marble Wildflower Wheat, Sandia Chile Grill Honey Wheat, Three Rivers Papa Bear's Golden Honey, Tractor Haymaker Honey Wheat.*

vegetable beers: *Back Alley Imperial Pumpkin Ale, Blue Corn Pumpkin Ale, Broken Bottle Debacle Pumpkin Ale, De La Vega's Pecan Amber Ale, La Cumbre Witch's Tit Pumpkin Ale, Mimbres Valley Foolish Fire Pumpkin Ale, Taos Ale House Cucurbita Imperial Pumpkin Ale, The Wellhead Bulldog Pumpkin Spice.*

INDEX

ABOUT THE AUTHOR

Jon C. Stott, Professor Emeritus of English, University of Alberta (Canada), spent nearly five decades of academic life writing textbooks and so-called scholarly studies. Since his retirement, he has been writing books about nonacademic things that interest him. These include four books on minor-league professional sports (*Leagues of Their Own*, McFarland, 2001; *Minor Leagues, Major Boom*, McFarland, 2004; *The Ice Men of Dixie*, Heritage House, 2006; and *Ice Warriors: The Pacific Coast/Western Hockey League, 1948–1974*, Heritage House, 2008). He has been studying beer in a very nonacademic, nonscientific way for more than half a century and is the author of *Beer Quest West: The Craft Brewers of Alberta and British Columbia* (Touchwood Editions, 2011). His blog www.beerquestwest.com includes essays about breweries and brewers, accounts of his beer travels and tasting notes. It will include periodic updates for *New Mexico Beer*. After having spent many winters in Albuquerque, avoiding the cold Canadian weather, he moved there permanently in 2013.

Visit us at
www.historypress.net
....

This title is also available as an e-book